GUI Design Essentials

Susan Weinschenk

Pamela Jamar

Sarah C. Yeo

Wiley Computer Publishing

John Wiley & Sons, Inc.

New York • Chichester • Weinheim • Brisbane • Toronto • Singapore

Executive Publisher: Katherine Schowalter

Editor: Theresa Hudson

Managing Editor: Mark Hayden

Electronic Products, Associate Editor: Mike Green

Text Design & Composition: SunCliff Graphic Productions

Designations used by companies to distinguish their products are often claimed as trademarks. In all instances where John Wiley & Sons, Inc. is aware of a claim, the product names appear in initial capital or ALL CAPITAL LETTERS. Readers, however, should contact the appropriate companies for more complete information regarding trademarks and registration.

This text is printed on acid-free paper.

This publication is designed to provide accurate and authoritative information in regard to the subject matter covered. It is sold with the understanding that the publisher is not engaged in rendering legal, accounting, or other professional service. If legal advice or other expert assistance is required, the services of a competent professional person should be sought.

Library of Congress Cataloging-in-Publication Data

Weinschenk, Susan.
    GUI design essentials for Windows 95, Windows 3.1 World Wide Web /
Susan Weinschenk, Pamela Jamar, Sarah C. Yeo.
      p.   cm.
    Includes index.
    ISBN 0-471-17549-8 (paper/CD-ROM : alk. paper)
    1. Graphical user interfaces (Computer systems)   2. Computer
software--Development. I. Jamar, Pamela. II. Yeo, Sarah C. III. Title
QA76.9.U83W4   1997
005.1'2--DC21   96-49769
                                               CIP

Printed in the United States of America

10 9 8 7 6 5 4 3 2 1

Dedicated to our families

Contents

PART I   THE PROCESS OF INTELLIGENT INTERFACE DESIGN   1

Chapter 1	An Overview of Intelligent Interface Design	3

Chapter 2	Analysis	13

Chapter 10   Presentation   213

Chapter 11   Internet and Intranet   237

Acknowledgments

We had lots of help on this book. Here are all the people we would like to thank:

Terri Hudson at Wiley for being interested in our subject, and all her work to get it out. Our clients and the readers of our first book *Guidelines for Enterprise-Wide GUI Design* (Wiley, 1995), who gave us valuable feedback on how to improve. Kelli Roddi for her insightful, thought-provoking conversations. Caryn Zange-Josephson and Kelley Schmidt for careful and valuable review of our text, pictures, concepts, and ideas. Linda Rothenberger for keeping us organized and stocked with lunch and snacks while we wrote and edited and wrote and edited and created and stored pictures. Sherry Servinsky for her hours and hours of work on the manuscript. Our families for their patience and support.

Preface

The question "Is it usable?" is being asked more and more frequently about software. A Fortune 1000 company called recently to say a mission-critical application had been pulled one month after it was installed because the users were in mutiny—all the features and functionality were there, but the new application made it harder to get their work done. It wasn't usable.

The interface is the part of the system that the user sees and interacts with. It is the part that is being judged as usable or not usable. Designing an interface that is easy to learn and use is related to, but different from, the design of the underlying software. Yet it is still common for the interface to receive very little attention during the development process. This is because development is such a huge effort, and there is so much pressure to perform quickly.

Ultimately, however, making computers easier to learn and use, and making them fit better to how real people perform their real work, means doing a better job of designing the system. That is what this book is all about.

We have some assumptions that permeate the book: We assume user-centered design. That is, we take as a beginning premise that you are designing for people; that humans are not perfect; that the computer software should be the one that has to adjust, not the person; that effective interface design processes must assume that we are designing to maximize the human's efficiency, not just the computer's efficiency.

We take as a beginning premise that to follow user-centered design means involving some users as an integral part of the design team;

that you will involve still more users by getting feedback from them; that you test your ideas iteratively and constantly with real users; that it is worth it to do the testing and revising because it will make the product better.

We take as a beginning premise that user-centered design does not mean abdicating responsibility for the usability of the interface; that it is not fair or effective to hand over interface design to the users; that it is not fair or effective to hand over interface design to the developers; that users and developers along with interface designers together design the interface; that no one group can do it alone.

We take as a beginning premise that user-centered design means that someone has to wear the usability or interface design hat on every project in order to ensure usable products.

We believe that the material in this book is valuable and will result in superior interfaces. But you need more. We are sometimes fascinated by the personalities of projects, organizations, and entire enterprises. Why is it that some organizations move forward and implement usable technology and others seem stuck? What are the organizational factors and people factors that are the underlying motivators? These motivators affect how people behave and thus how they design software and software interfaces. Below are our suggested practices for facilitating the development of usable technology:

- ❏ *Stop projects in trouble.* The willingness and empowerment to stop projects, whether the trouble is budget, time, scope, or resources, seems to be critical. You are only wasting time and money by continuing to try and save technology projects that are in real trouble. Successful technology organizations put a halt on them until they can regroup and either radically intervene or start over. Though the consequences of that seem large they are nothing compared with the consequences of moving forward to disaster.

- ❏ *Don't look to technology for salvation.* In his book *The Secrets of Consulting* (Dorset House, 1985), Gerald Weinberg says that all technology problems are really people problems. If you have a problem look to people for a solution. The technology is just a tool for the people who are really doing the work and the saving. Technology alone won't save you or the organization. Faster machines or new programming tools alone are not the answer.

❏ *Employ reasonable deadlines.* If you want to guarantee *unusable* technology, then give everyone an impossible deadline. Then tell them on top of that they *have* to have it done by second quarter no matter what. You will not get what you need. Everyone will have to cut corners. It's not what you really want.

❏ *Put the right people on mission-critical projects.* You will have to commit the time and resources of your best people to work on these projects. Not your best technology people—your best regular people. The ones who do the actual work. Give them time and access to the resources they need. They are the driving force that will get it right. Don't expect them to do their normal work *while they are on the special project.*

❏ *Do a lot of the work yourself.* Don't bring in the experts to do it all. Your own people know your business and have to be in the forefront. You can give your people help. Use experts for guidance and for small pieces. Use outsourcing wisely, but don't turn your project over entirely to someone on the outside.

❏ *Take the time to do it right.* Be patient. When you are looking for a better way to do something, there is a lot of not very exciting work that is the truly valuable work: Documenting how people currently do their work. Deciding how it could be changed. Deciding what is a manageable piece to work on. Researching and evaluating what technology tools are really available. Documenting the details of how you want the solution to blend in with the new work. Designing the interface, redesigning, testing it out, redesigning, implementing, changing. and so on takes time. You need a small team committed to working on the project. The team must have the responsibility and authority to get it done and the time to do it right. The team must be allowed to experiment, investigate, try things out, make mistakes, start again. The end result is worth it.

How did we help that Fortune 1000 company that had to pull its software? We used two basic tactics of good interface design:

❏ An effective interface design process—an effective process guides you to ask the right questions, answer them realistically, document the answers, and get feedback from others that you are on the right track. An effective process makes it easy to design iteratively.

❏ Effective guidelines—guidelines ensure you are following the basic principles of usable interface design, creating interfaces that are consistent and intuitive.

Part I of the book describes in detail the process we follow in doing Intelligent Interface Design. This is by no means the only way to do interface design, but rather a compilation of phases, steps, forms, and ideas that have worked for us. The CD-ROM that accompanies this book contains many of the forms and examples we use in the book.

Part II of the book contains interface design guidelines. This is an updated version of our first book, *Guidelines for Enterprise-Wide GUI Design*. It contains Windows 95 guidelines as well as Internet and Intranet guidelines. The CD-ROM portion for Part II contains:

❏ The book in an online format you can read on a computer.
❏ The book in electronic form that you can customize as you need to create your own enterprise-wide guidelines.

Software projects are under so much stress. There are new tools, impossible deadlines, technical people to train . . . promoting and maintaining usability is not always easy with the flurry of activities that accompanies the design and development of a large software project. We hope that this book can help you reach your usability goals.

The Authors

GUI Design
Essentials

PART I

The Process of Intelligent Interface Design

Chapter 1

An Overview of Intelligent Interface Design

Analysis	Design	Construction
Identify Scope	Choose Objects	Develop Prototype
Develop User Profiles	Select Metaphors	Test Prototype
Gather Data	Storyboard	Document the Design
Document Current Tasks	Create High Level Design	
Document Opportunities	Test	
Describe Future Tasks	Develop Support Plan	
Develop Usability Specs		
Develop Scenarios		
Test		

Contents

A Tale of Two Software Projects

Here is a true story about two software projects. One ended in failure and the other in success. These are true stories, but we changed the names of the organizations, individuals, and products.

Project A: TransOnline

Acme Insurance was nearing the release of Phase I of their new product, TransOnline, a new system for processing insurance transactions online. George was one of the project team members, and he had become concerned about the usability of the interface. He felt confident about the functionality and features of the software—Acme Insurance had conducted some analysis to determine what their users wanted the system to do. But he was concerned that the design of the interface was far from optimal, that users would become frustrated using the software, would not realize its capabilities, and would make errors on critical transactions.

Most of the programmers on the team did not think the problems with the interface were that severe. They had followed standard Windows guidelines, more or less, and were concentrating on writing code and maximizing the efficiency and speed of the transactions. No specific interface design activities had been performed on the project, nor was an interface design process followed. The development team went from their requirements document into system design, and then into prototyping and coding of the system.

As the project got closer to its beta deadline date, George became more and more worried. He requested that a usability test be performed on the prototype. At first the other team members and key stakeholders resisted the idea, feeling that it was a distraction to the deadline date and an unnecessary use of time and money. George finally got a go-ahead to conduct a usability test—partly because he eventually convinced some people, and partly because people were tired of his talking about interface problems.

With help from some of the team, George planned and conducted the test, and analyzed and presented the results to the entire team and key stakeholders. George was correct. In the usability test, real users had great difficulty in performing several of the tasks. The problems they had were severe, and in many cases resulted in their not being able to process transactions at all, or, even worse, the users thought they had processed transactions correctly and had not.

George made recommendations for changes to the interface. Some of the changes were small ones, for example changing the name of a command button (small change, big impact), changing the type of control used, or the order in which items appear on a drop-down menu. Other changes were far more extensive, however, and affected the structure of the interface. For example, in many parts of the software, the flow of windows and screens did not match the way the users needed to perform the task.

When the project managers analyzed how much rework was necessary, the deadline date for the beta was pulled. Major redesign of the interface and software began. Because the code had been written before the usability test, changes in the interface design caused massive rewrites of code. One year later the beta version was still not released.

The system had been two years in development before the usability test. Another year of changes and development occurred after that. As of this writing there are serious doubts as to whether the system will be released at all.

Project B: UniCall

UCallUs, a large communications company, was at the beginning of a new client server project—UniCall, a call center application. It was an important project, and they were relatively new to client server design and development, so they decided to do some research and investigation before starting to write code.

Elizabeth, a member of the IS staff, was asked to join a task force looking into best practices for GUI design and development. One of the areas the task force decided to investigate was interface design, and Elizabeth was assigned to learn about incorporating interface design processes into their software projects.

An interface design plan was created for the project that was separate from, but related to and coordinated with, the software development part of the project. A team of developers, users, and business unit representatives documented detailed profiles of the users and task flows of how they worked in the call center now and would work with the new system.

Before they began drawing screens, the team made some decisions about overall interface design. They tried out different models and metaphors, and different ways to present the objects and actions to users.

Having iterated some initial ideas, the team developed a mockup of their design. The mockup was designed to match the way the users needed to do their work. The design team showed the mockup to users and key stakeholders. Some of the windows were confusing or hard to use. The team revised them, showed them again, and made another round of revisions.

They showed the mockup to some of the technical people and they discussed the technical impact of some of the design decisions. As a result they made some more revisions. They then conducted usability tests of the mockup with real users, and made further revisions.

Because their design reviews and testing were done so early in the process, however, the changes were easy to make. Each time they got feedback from others, the comments and revisions became smaller and smaller in scope. They did not have to do massive redesigns, but instead refined the design they had.

Next, the design team created a detailed computer prototype. They went through a round of reviews, revisions, and usability testing with the prototype, and made a last set of changes to the design before they started developing the actual software.

The total amount of elapsed time from the time the team started to the end of the computer prototype was nine months. During this time the software development team was doing their own analysis work so that they would be ready when the interface was ready. In January, the interface was completed and given to the development team to work on. On June 15 of the same year, the system was rolled out, on time and on budget. Very few interface changes were required between January and June—all stakeholders and users knew what the system was going to look and feel like beforehand. They had had time to give their feedback and make changes. The software development team could work on implementing a design that was not continually shifting underneath them. When the system was delivered it matched the plan for how everyone would work in the new call center. Costly modifications during and after development were avoided.

The major difference between the two projects is that the UniCall project followed a process of Intelligent Interface Design and the Trans-Online project did not. In Part I we cover the process of Intelligent Interface Design—what it is and how to do it.

What Is an Interface?

A software interface is the part of an application that the user sees and interacts with. It is related to, but not the same as, the underlying structure, architecture, and code that makes the software work. The interface includes the screens, windows, controls, menus, metaphors, online help, documentation, and training. Anything the user sees and interacts with is part of the interface.

Why Intelligent Interface Design?

From the user's point of view, the interface *is* the software.

There is a body of knowledge about how people think, learn, and work. Intelligent Interface Design taps into that body of knowledge and applies it to the design of a software interface.

An intelligent interface is easy to learn and use. It allows users to do their work or perform a task in the way that makes the most sense to them, rather than having to adjust to the software. An intelligent interface is specifically designed for the people who will be using it. It maximizes what we know about human strengths, for example, analysis and decision making, and minimizes what we know are human limitations, for example, memory and complex computations. It takes the environment, tasks, and experience of the people using the product into account in its design.

Well-designed interfaces reduce errors, training time and costs, make people more productive, result in superior customer service, and get used. With Intelligent Interface Design you can improve software, save money on reworks, and get the interface right the first time.

"THERE'S NOTHING WRONG WITH THE SYSTEM; THEREFORE, WE'LL NEED TO PERFORM EXPLORATORY BRAIN SURGERY ON YOU."

If faced with fixing the interface or fixing the person, opt for the interface.

Why an Interface Design Process?

Many fields and disciplines have a history of applying design techniques to improve human use of an object or technology. There are design principles and processes for creating books and magazines, airplane cockpits, copy machines, and telephones. There are design processes for designing and developing effective, efficient software. There are also processes and best practices for designing effective and efficient interfaces.

As interfaces have grown, changed, matured, and changed some more, the process by which they are created and applied has also matured and become more sophisticated. Some people think that interface design is a new field, born out of graphical user interfaces. Actually the field goes back at least as far as World War II—with the design of airplane cockpits. Many of those early interfaces were not computer software interfaces, but hardware interfaces. As computers came more and more out of the lab and into the world of work, however, the role of interface design began to expand.

The authors of this book have each been working in the field of interface design for over 16 years. This means that our experience of interface design goes back at least to character-based, alphanumeric interfaces. (If we mention the teletype-style interfaces and punch cards we will really date ourselves!)

Some people think that interface design becomes less and less necessary as the interfaces we have to work with evolve and become somewhat standardized. The opposite is true: As interfaces become richer in possibilities, more graphical, and offer more choices for both the developers and the users, the importance of interface design increases. There is also the users' expectation that computers will become even easier to learn and use.

In Part I we have compiled all the best practices we have learned over the last 16 years. We do not mean to imply that these are the only good processes and tools to use. We have documented what works well for us. These are the phases and steps we follow as we work with clients on large and small user interface projects. We have attempted to explain them in a practical way so that you can take them and use them as is, or adapt them within your own organization. To that end, we have included forms and checklists both in the text and on the accompanying CD-ROM.

The Three Phases of Interface Design

We have divided the whole process of intelligent interface design into three phases: Analysis, Design, and Construction, as shown in Figure 1.1.

Although these names can also be used to refer to software development, they have different meanings and different steps when referring to interface design.

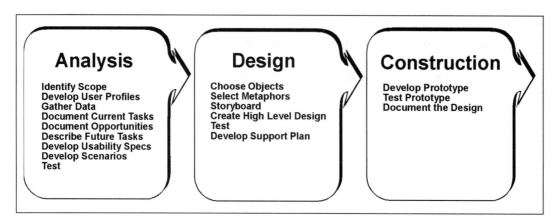

Figure 1.1 The phases of Intelligent Interface Design.

Analysis

In the Analysis phase of Intelligent Interface Design, you analyze what you know about the people who will be using the interface you are designing. You analyze and document who they are, how they work now, and how you expect them to work in the future when they have the software whose interface you are designing.

When you complete analysis, you have a complete picture of the requirements for the interface. (Reminder: not the requirements for the software, but for the interface).

In our experience, analysis for interface design is often scantily done, or not done at all. If you don't have this critical information about users and how they work now, and how they will work with the new software, how can you design an interface that will be easy to learn and use? Without this critical information up front you end up reworking and reworking the design. If you do not spend some time and money up front, you will spend 10 times as much later on.

Design

In the Design phase of Intelligent Interface Design, you take all the information from Analysis and apply it to shape an interface. Although design involves a fair amount of creative brain power, it is not a freeform creative process. The process we describe shows you how to take the time-based (temporal) tasks you study in analysis, and out of these, extract a structure that works for that particular set of users, the tasks they perform, the environment they work in, and the constraints of the project. You are not designing the software structure, but the interface structure, in other words, the interface objects that the user will manipulate, and the actions they will take on those objects as they perform their work.

Construction

By construction we don't mean constructing the software, we mean constructing the interface. It is during construction that you create a prototype of the interface, revise it, test it thoroughly for usability problems, revise again, and document the prototype in detail so that the development team can implement it.

Supporting Chapters

Analysis, Design, and Construction are the three main phases of Intelligent Interface Design. Each of these phases has its own chapter in Part I. Testing is included in each of the three phases, but a separate chapter, "Usability Testing," describes different methods and steps for performing a test.

There are many similarities between interface design for GUI projects and designing Web sites, but there are some differences. We have described these in a chapter entitled "Designing for the Web."

Interface Design Is not a Search for the Holy Grail

For a particular group of users trying to perform a particular set of tasks with a particular interface there is no one perfect interface waiting to be found. Interface design is not the search for the holy grail. There are as many different design solutions as there are design teams.

But, not all interface designs are equally usable. It is our plan and hope that the ideas, tools, techniques, and processes described in Part I will help you in your search for a highly usable interface.

Chapter 2

Analysis

Analysis	Design	Construction
Identify Scope **Develop User Profiles** **Gather Data** **Document Current Tasks** **Document Opportunities** **Describe Future Tasks** **Develop Usability Specs** **Develop Scenarios** **Test**	Choose Objects Select Metaphors Storyboard Create High Level Design Test Develop Support Plan	Develop Prototype Test Prototype Document the Design

Contents

Purpose

Deliverables

Preparation

Process

Summary

13

A common reason users find an interface unfriendly or not intuitive is because it does not support how they really do their work and think about their work. Too often, the software architecture design dictates the interface design, for example, logical system function partitioning and data flow dictate screen or window partitioning and dialog flow.

Analysis identifies current user tasks and the information, concepts, and terminology users use when performing their work. It then describes future tasks from which the interface design work can begin. Analysis is a key phase in designing an interface that is an effective tool for users.

In this chapter we will explore the steps in analysis using a sample application, Check-Ease, software for keeping an individual's checkbook on computer.

Purpose

The purpose of the Analysis phase is to document and verify information about the users, their current work, and the vision of their work when the new software is in place. This information feeds directly into the next phase, Design.

Deliverables

Deliverables in this phase include:

- ❑ *User profiles.* A complete description of your primary and secondary users.
- ❑ *Current task analyses.* Thorough descriptions of how users are currently doing their work.
- ❑ *Future task descriptions.* High-level descriptions of how users will be doing their work using the new software.
- ❑ *Usability specifications.* Identification of which usability issues and areas are of most concern for this project and specific measurements to determine whether the resulting software is usable.
- ❑ *Use case scenarios.* A set of specific scenarios for how users will interact with the new software, for use in the next phase, Design.

Preparation

Before you begin analysis, you should put together an analysis team consisting of:

❑ *One interface designer.* This person is the one who most needs to use the analysis results. Because of this, he or she will make sure the work stays focused and in the right amount of detail.

❑ *Two content experts/users.* Since you are describing the way users will work in detail, it is critical that you have people present who can really describe the work on a detailed level. You want more than one content expert/user because often the best information comes out of listening to two users talk to each other. During the part of analysis where you describe the future, it is important that the users be knowledgeable about future plans and have the authority to say how the tasks will or should be done.

❑ *One technical person.* You may not need to have a technical person involved in all the working sessions for analysis, but you should have one identified that is available to answer questions as they arise about planned system opportunities and constraints.

❑ *A managerial-level person.* If a manager would be helpful in answering questions for a particular step you should have one there. There may be times, however, when including the manager may prevent your users from talking freely. You may need to have some sessions without a manager present.

Process

The Analysis phase includes both learning about and documenting users' current tasks, as well as documenting and verifying the future tasks from the user's point of view.

The steps in the Analysis phase are:

1. Identify current state and scope.
2. Develop user profiles.
3. Gather data.

4. Document current tasks.
5. Document problems and opportunities.
6. Describe future tasks.
7. Develop usability specifications.
8. Develop use case scenarios.
9. Test.

Identify Current State and Scope

You are probably not the first person to do analysis work for a particular project. It is important, therefore, for you to know what has and has not been done, especially in the area of analysis. You do not want to redo work or be redundant with information that has already been gathered. On the other hand, be careful about assuming that someone else has documented users' work thoroughly. Our experience shows that there is a lot of variability in both the quantity and quality of analysis work that is actually completed on a project.

Consider Work in Progress

You will want to study and/or review any materials on the project that are available. Has there been a feasibility study? A meeting to discuss the new system? Business process reengineering?

Make sure you know what work has been done, and at what stage the project is. It is possible that some of the materials you need or even would be creating for analysis have already been completed, or at least started. If you find some already completed, verify that the information is still valid.

Decide on the Scope of the Analysis

Define the scope of the analysis in terms of the user activities the interface will support and portray. The goal is to identify the high-level task areas, not the flow or steps involved in performing the tasks. Detailed analysis of the current tasks will be performed later, as part of the Document Current Tasks step.

Consider the following as you decide on the scope of the analysis:

❏ Consult project documentation and project management to identify the general user activities that the new interface will support. User activities are high-level task areas. For example, for an electronic checkbook application these might be: Write Checks, Balance Checkbook, Record Deposits, and so on.

❏ List and describe briefly the user activities identified.

❏ Check the list of activities to make sure that the perspective and wording reflect user activities. There will be other system functions required to support the user in performing these activities, but the focus here is on what users do.

❏ If an activity is very broad, list user tasks that are performed as part of the activity. For example, for a personal information manager application, the activity Maintain Personal Calendar would include the tasks Enter Appointments and Move/Change Appointments.

❏ Check that the activity and task wording is independent of interface design solutions or assumptions, for instance Find A Check, not Scroll Through Register.

❏ Make sure that the wording doesn't refer to the current system design, for instance, Set Up New Client Service, not Enter an IN Order.

The list of activities and tasks represents starting assumptions about the scope of the interface and the analysis work. These assumptions and any outstanding issues should be reviewed with the rest of the project team.

Define Interface Design Constraints

In an ideal project, all decisions regarding the design and implementation of the interface would be driven by user needs. Unfortunately, in real-world projects, technology, business concerns, and other system issues place constraints on the interface design. Your objective is to identify all system hardware, software, and project features and requirements that might constrain the interface design:

❏ Consult work in progress to identify decisions that have already been made regarding hardware, software and project constraints.

❑ Identify the interface technology that will be employed, for example, GUI, a mixture of GUI and 3270 screens, and so on.

❑ Identify the platforms (for example, UNIX, DOS, OS/2) and machines (for example, UNIX workstations, X terminals, PCs) that will be used.

❑ Identify what user interface techniques will be available. For example, is this a multiple window environment? Will all users have display hardware that supports color? What are the available text fonts? Will all users have a keyboard with function keys, a mouse, a trackball?

❑ Identify any corporate or project interface design standards and style guides that are to be followed (such as IBM Common User Access, Microsoft Windows, Open Look).

❑ Identify the degree of distributive processing. How much functionality will be performed by the user interface (for example, edits, computations)? How will this affect user interaction (for example, system response time)?

Document these interface design constraints. They represent a set of starting interface design assumptions. Review the constraints and any outstanding issues regarding interface technology and implementation with the rest of the project team.

Figure 2.1 shows the interface design constraints for the Check-Ease application.

Interface Design Constraints for Check-Ease

IBM PC 486 or better (and clones). More and more, these will be laptop computers.

Modems with baud rates as low as 14400.

EGA and VGA monitors. Minimum resolution is 640 x 480.

Color and monochrome displays.

Microsoft Windows 95 compliance or better.

Figure 2.1 Design constraints for Check-Ease.

Develop User Profiles

A common mistake designers make is to assume that all users are like themselves. Then they design for themselves. When designing software for the nonprogrammer, most software designers/developers are not representative of their users. Two other reasons that interface designers are sometimes in the dark about users:

❏ They are not given the opportunity and resources to study users.

❏ Marketing or management doesn't want to get pinned down on the precise targets for the system.

It is not possible to design a user-friendly interface without designing for a user. It is not possible to design for no one nor to design for everyone. Building a description of target users is the first, and a critical, step in interface design.

To be useful for interface design, user profiles must go beyond simple characterizations like computer novices, computer experts, managers, or secretaries. The objective is to find out about those user characteristics that will be most important for interface design trade-offs. These include:

❏ *User experience with the hardware and software environments that the project will use.* What percent of target users are now using a mouse? What percent are keyboard touch typists familiar with standard keyboard layout? What percent are now using windowed interfaces? Are the interfaces these users are familiar with compliant with any standard styles like Microsoft Windows?

❏ *User experience with the kind of software application the project will develop.* Will this be their first application of this type (for example, first accounting application)? If not, which systems are they now using?

❏ *User task experience/expertise.* Have these users performed this kind of work before?

❏ *Expected frequency of use and job turnover.* If turnover is very high or frequency of use will be very low, the users will never become experts at the software. Therefore interface ease of learning will be important. If frequency of use will be very high and turnover will be low, ease of use will be more important than ease of learning.

A completed user profile is shown in Figure 2.2. Note that key interface design requirements are listed at the bottom of the profile.

How are user profiles different from marketing analyses? Marketing information and discussions with field representatives are often good places to start when building user profiles. However, they often contain information that is not critical to designing an interface, and may be missing some detailed information that is needed for interface design. You may need to supplement marketing information with user interviews and/or surveys in order to obtain and validate all the required data.

"But, we can't build a user profile, we have too many kinds of users." Designing for everyone is designing for no one. If the system will support multiple, very different groups of users, then user profiles must be developed for at least the key groups. Estimate what percentage of the total users each group represents. These numbers will be critical when trading off interface design approaches and features.

To develop user profiles:

❑ Work with project management and project marketing to identify targeted user groups for the system and its interface.

❑ Work with marketing, field representatives, and representative users to develop draft descriptions of targeted user groups.

❑ Identify user experience with the hardware environment that will be used (for example, IBM PC, SUN, networking) and input and output devices that will be used (for example, mouse experience, keyboard typing skills).

❑ Identify user experience with the software environment that will be used (such as windowed user interfaces in general, specific interface style such as Microsoft Windows 95, and so on.).

❑ Identify user experience with similar software applications (for example, other financial software, other accounting packages, and so on.).

❑ Identify user experience with the actual work and tasks that the application will support (such as accounting, financial planning, and so on.).

❑ Characterize targeted users on other dimensions that could be important for interface design, including frequency of use, rate of turnover, level of motivation in using the system, discretionary versus mandatory system usage, and multilinguism.

User Profile

Application: Checkbook for IBM PCs and PC clones

Potential Users: Adults who currently have an IBM PC or PC clone, Microsoft Windows 95, and a checking account at a bank.

Hardware Experience:

- 100% currently have an IBM PC or PC clone; that is, users will not be purchasing a computer for this application.
- 100% will have a mouse or trackball.

Software and Interface Experience:

- Over 90% are using a Microsoft Windows 95 application now such as a word processing or a spreadsheet application; that is, users will not be purchasing and learning Windows 95 for this application.
- Less than 50% have used a modem before.

Experience with Similar Applications: Less than 15% are currently using another electronic checkbook application.

Task Experience:

- All currently have a checking account at a bank.
- Only 40% probably balance a checkbook now; users are not bankers or accountants.
- Less than 10% do any electronic banking from home now.

Frequency of Use: Frequency of use will be very low (every couple of months) to low (twice a month).

Key Interface Design Requirements that Profile Suggests:

- Conformance to Windows 95 interface style
- Ease of learning will be important
- Build on existing mental model of manual checking
- Provide an intuitive model for modem aspects
- Do not assume good understanding of procedures for balancing a checkbook

Figure 2.2 Sample user profile form.

❏ Where needed, for each of these characteristics identify and estimate size of user subgroups in percentages (for example, 25% using interface now, 50% used interface a few times, 25% never used interface before).

❏ Validate these draft profiles through user questionnaire surveys, interviews, and site visits.

❏ Identify key interface design requirements that these profiles suggest (such as compatibility with existing interface standards, compatibility with current/existing applications, ease of use versus ease of learning).

❏ Everyone on the design team, in development, and in marketing needs to agree on who the interface is for before you start designing it (shared vision). Make sure there is good understanding and consensus.

❏ Document user profiles and other interface design requirements. Otherwise, how will you defend the design the first time a project manager (who is not a target user) tries the interface and declares it unfriendly?

❏ Use the user profiles to determine who to interview and observe during the rest of the Analysis phase, and who would be appropriate users for design reviews and usability testing in future phases.

Gather Data

Once you have identified who your users are, you need to gather data from them. The data you are gathering includes verifying your user profiles, as well as getting details on their current and future task flows. To provide the critical data needed for interface design, task descriptions must be built by talking to and observing users who do the work the system is targeted to support, not from talking to managers, marketing representatives, trainers, and so on. There are several methods you can use to gather data. Three are described below.

Bringing Users In

One of the most common ways that information is gathered is by bringing users in to your work place and asking them questions about their work. This is usually a convenient and cost-effective way for you to gather data, and it can yield some valuable information, but it has some dangers and drawbacks that you want to watch out for:

❏ *Oversimplification.* If users feel you are not a domain expert, they will often try to be helpful by oversimplifying the description of their work. They may not realize that this is not helpful, but actually harmful to your data collection. And if you are, indeed, lacking in domain expertise, you may not realize at all that you don't have the full picture. These can lead to important tasks not being captured in enough detail later when you need to create a current task analysis or future task description.

❏ *Missing information.* Have you ever tried to describe in words a task that you do out of context? It can be difficult to remember or to describe everything in the right order. Yet this is what you are asking users to do when you bring them in away from their work and then expect them to describe what they do. You can also miss important information if you do not see their artifacts (artifacts are the physical objects they manipulate in their real environment, for example, forms, cards, folders, maps). These artifacts contain important information about how users do their work. When users are out of their own environment and context they may forget to mention some artifacts, or you may not understand exactly what they mean by just having them described.

❏ *Too much detail.* When users are interviewed out of context it is hard for you to know if you are getting the appropriate level of detail. You might be getting more than you actually need in order to complete your task analysis.

❏ *Misunderstanding.* Because the interview is out of context it is easy for you to misunderstand some of the information you are getting. For example, your user may say that she gets calls from customers on the phone. You may not realize that the user doesn't actually take the call, but gets a summary message.

Since interviewing users in your office and out of context has these problems, you may want to avoid this technique in favor of the contextual methods described later, or at least combine this method with others.

Role Playing

Another way to get information from users is to role play with them. If they are customer service representatives, pretend you are a customer and role play what their interaction would be like. This role playing will yield some additional and more realistic information than just asking them questions about how they would interact with a real customer. It is still a far cry, however, from actually observing a real interaction, and will therefore have the same drawbacks as bringing users in for interviews.

Field Studies

Field studies involve going to the users' workplace and observing real users. Field studies are the most powerful way to gather useful and important data quickly. They also allow you to see the context of people's work, for example, the physical environment, amount of stress or distraction, noise and light levels, and so on. There are always surprises when you go out and watch users in the field, and because of this it is almost always worth the extra time and/or expense that field studies might entail. There are many interface designers that say they cannot design a usable system if they cannot conduct at least one field study.

Here are some considerations in planning and conducting a field study:

- ❑ *Decide on the purpose of your visit.* Decide ahead of time what you want to capture. Are you looking for details on specific tasks the users perform? Are you verifying the user profiles? Do you want to collect artifacts from the user's real world? Are you just trying to get a feel for the users and the work they do? All of these are valid reasons for conducting a field study, but you need to get specific about the visit so that you can prepare any materials you need to bring with you or bring back.

- ❑ *Plan your interviews and data collection.* Given your purpose in visiting, how will you collect your data? Are you going to conduct a formal interview? Have users fill out surveys? Have an informal discussion? Watch as much as possible without interrupting? Although you should build in unplanned time just to see what the user's world is all about, make sure you do some planning so you can collect the information you really need. What do you need to bring with you? What do you need to bring back from the user's site?

❑ *Make sure you are expected and preapproved.* Don't just show up on site and expect to be taken care of. Make sure you have set up your visit ahead of time, including arranging with the users' manager and scheduling time that works for the users with minimal disruption of their work. Also make sure the tasks you want to see are actually going to occur during the time you plan on visiting. Obtain any necessary written permissions ahead of time, for example, being able to videotape, or take materials with you. Make sure the users know you are coming, not just the manager. If you can, speak ahead of time by phone to the actual users you are meeting with.

❑ *Consider a partner.* Consider working with a partner during site visits. That way one of you can be taking notes while the other one observes or interviews. Or one can be operating the video camera while the other one interviews.

❑ *Consider video- or audiotaping.* Videotaping can be a big plus if you are alone since you don't have to worry about missing crucial information, or reading your notes afterwards. Remember, however, that it can take a long time to pour through video afterwards. Consider videotaping just some of the meetings, or videotaping the physical environment. Consider audiotaping instead. It is not as powerful as video, but it is easier to do and your users will not feel as intimidated by an audiorecorder.

❑ *Leave time.*   Leave plenty of time for questions when you are on site. Make sure you have time between users to write down your comments when you are alone. Schedule enough time with the users to ask them questions on what you observed.

❑ *Consider role playing during the visit.* If you can't observe an actual task while you are onsite (for example no one calls that day with the kind of problem you wanted to capture the user responding to), ask the user to role play the task with you.

❑ *Make the users comfortable.* People are often nervous about being watched. Build rapport before you begin the session. Introduce yourself and your partner, explain what you are doing and why.

Make sure they know they can stop or take breaks whenever they need to.

❑ *Just watch.* Sometimes it is tempting to start designing the new interface while you are watching the user use the old one. Stifle this desire. Your job during a field study is to observe and collect data, not analyze and design. If you have an idea, jot it down and then forget about it until later.

Document the Current Tasks

Documenting the current tasks involves looking at how users do their work now in enough detail to provide the data you need to design a new interface. Task analysis provides important clues to what the interface organization and conceptual design should be. Of course, where possible, the new system and interface should *improve* on how users currently perform their tasks. This new vision is documented in later steps (Describe Future Tasks and Create Use Case Scenarios). But first, it is critical to clearly understand the mental models users will bring with them to the new system. Users have built up certain ways of thinking about their work and you need to study and document these mental models, and take them into account when you design.

Describe each task

For each user task, document the following information:

❑ The actual task performed
❑ Tasks that precede, follow, or interrupt the task (task flow)
❑ Interdependencies with other tasks, flexibility of task orders
❑ The frequency with which the task is performed
❑ Which users perform task
❑ Information display requirements (What information do users see when performing the task?)
❑ Input requirements (What do users enter?)
❑ Task support (What other documents and tools do they use when performing this task?)
❑ Task products and where they go

- Common task performance problems, errors
- Terminology and concepts users use when describing and performing the task
- Users' complaints about how the task is performed today and their ideas about how task performance could be improved
- Characteristics of the work environment where the task is performed (for example, small, cluttered, dirty workspace that would make mouse use difficult)

Task analysis is about learning what users do, not asking users to design the interface. Task analysis only asks users for what they know best: their expertise on performing their work. The interface designer doesn't ask, "Do you need windows?" Through task analysis, the interface designer translates a requirement like, "I need to see these three kinds of information at the same time," into an interface design requirement for multiwindowed display.

Task analysis describes user tasks from the user's perspective, not the system functional or architecture perspective, and independently of any interface screen design concepts. Documenting the current tasks means describing how the work is done now, before the new system is in place.

Document the Current Tasks

You have several choices for how to document current tasks: task charts, task detail tables, and task sketches.

Task charts show in great detail the tasks that the users currently follow. One of the main reasons that new interfaces fail is because they don't meet the needs of complex users performing complex, real-world tasks. A common lack in current analysis practices (where they exist at all) is to oversimplify the picture of how users perform current tasks, and/or to not document all the tasks or all the contingencies. Although it is important during the next phase, Design, to design with common and frequent flow in mind, that does not mean that exceptions or less frequent tasks or branches can be ignored.

It is critical, therefore, that your current task description be detailed and thorough. Task charts are good tools for beginning to capture that detail.

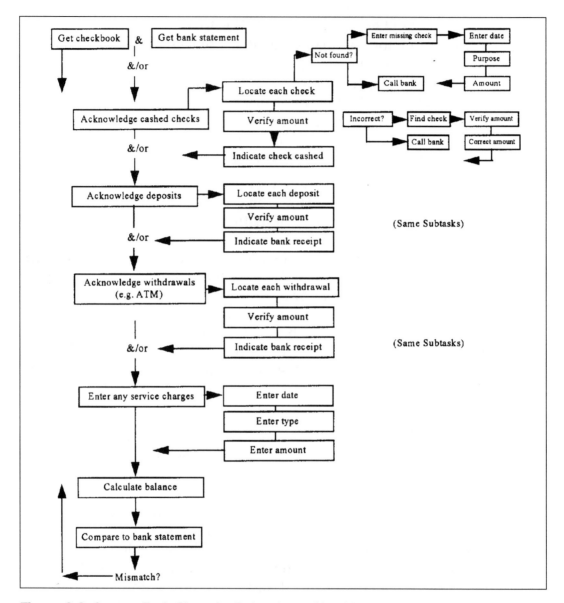

Figure 2.3 Current Task Chart for Balancing a Checkbook.

Figure 2.3 shows part of the Task Chart for Balancing the Checkbook from our checkbook case study.

Task charts show a lot of detail, but the use of diagrams and boxes limits the amount of text that can be included. Task detail tables allow

Task #	Task	Frequency	Display Requirements	Input Requirements	Comments
1.0	Acknowledge Checks				
1.1	Locate check	High	Check number Date Purpose Amount Statement	Navigate to check	Statement ordered by check number, users may search on other parameters. Do all banks use format: date-no.-amount?
1.1.1	Enter missing	Low-moderate	Entry feedback	Check number Date Purpose Amount Indicate cashed	Users will want placed in numeric order
1.2	Verify	High	Same as 1.1	None	
1.3	Indicate check cashed	High	Same as 1.1. Cashed indicator	Cashed state	Users will need to remove as well
(etc.)					

Figure 2.4 Part of the Current Task Detail table for Balancing a Checkbook.

you to thoroughly capture and document all the data you will need to create a new interface. Figure 2.4 shows part of the Task Detail Table for the Task Chart you saw above.

The columns in the task detail table allow you to note how often users perform the step (Frequency), what the user needs to see to complete the step (Display Requirements), what the user enters (Input Requirements), and very importantly, a comments column where you can annotate problems with the current task flow and ideas for changes as the new interface is designed. Figure 2.5 shows part of the Task Detail Table for Paying Bills.

In contrast to task charts and task detail tables, task sketches show a high-level view of the current flow of work for a particular group of users performing a task or set of tasks. Figure 2.6 shows the Task Sketch that describes just one common path through the task of Paying Bills.

Task #	Task	Frequency	Display Requirements	Input Requirements	Comments
1.1	Get checkbook	High			
1.2	Get bills	High			
1.3	Add up bills and compare with current funds	High	View current balance and total of bills	Add each bill amount, subtract from current balance	If user can't find calculator, need to do it by hand
1.4	Decide if there are enough funds to pay all bills	High	View current balance minus total of bills		
1.5	If there aren't enough funds, decide how much to pay on each bill to balance with current funds	Low	View current balance and total of bills	Add new amount of bills, subtract from current balance	Tedious—calculate and recalculate the balance
1.6	Write checks	High	View checks and bills	Write date, payee, numerical dollar amount, text dollar amount, signature, and note	
1.7	Enter checks in register	High	View checks and register	Write check number, date, payee, and amount	Redundancy—write out checks and write them in register
1.8	Calculate new balance	High	View register	Subtract each entry from current balance	

Figure 2.5 Current Task Detail table for part of Paying Bills.

Notice that these sketches are high-level. They lack the detail of the task charts and task detail tables. They are useful, however, in summarizing the task at a high level, and also have the added advan-

Figure 2.6 Current Task Sketch for Paying Bills.

tage of showing in a visual way the environment and location of the user when tasks are being performed.

All of these techniques can be used on manual tasks that are to be computerized, tasks that are part manual/part computerized now, or tasks that are currently computerized, and will be updated with a new system.

During your data gathering you should have collected artifacts, or real-life pieces of people's work. For example, you could bring back lists, reports, memos, an example file, anything that helps you remember and describe the user's actual work.

For Check-Ease data gathering we brought back samples of bank statements, checks, checkbook registers, and bills to be paid.

Document Problems and Opportunities

After you have documented how work is currently done, you are ready to describe the changes to be made. There are many sources for the changes that you want to incorporate, for example, information from feasibility work or problems or opportunities you uncovered while you were documenting the current task analysis. Figure 2.7 shows possible sources for problems and opportunities. Gather all these problems and opportunities in one place. You may want to group them into categories and put labels on the categories (for example, Performance Issues, Frustrations, and so on).

For example, we found the problems and opportunities shown in Figure 2.8 for the current method of Paying Bills.

You want to make sure to use all the valuable information that you have collected. It is critical that you use the current state as the starting point when making decisions on how the future should be. In order to do this, you will want to connect the current state with problems and opportunities for change so you know where to consider making changes. Consider creating a map to the future by putting each change or opportunity on a sticky note and attaching it to the place on the current task sketch or task chart where it belongs. One problem or opportunity might come up in more than one place. Put them wherever they fit, as many times as is appropriate.

Figure 2.9 shows the current Task Sketch for Paying Bills with the problems and opportunities attached where they belong.

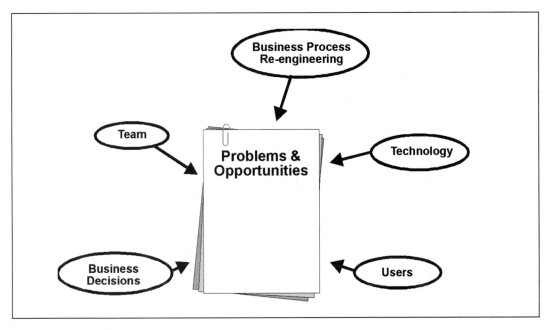

Figure 2.7 Problems and opportunities can come from many different sources.

Problems and Opportunities List for Current Task of Paying Bills

Can't find calculator, must add/subtract in head or with paper and pencil.

Current balance might not be up to date, have to stop and calculate.

Error prone—relies on correct calculations.

Tedious to calculate and recalculate the running balance.

Handwriting is bad, people may read wrong amounts on checks.

Redundancy—write check and then repeat all the information in check register.

Would be nice to have tracking of what has been spent for different categories (such as food, medical, and so on).

More work to get an updated balance.

Figure 2.8 List of problems and opportunities for task of paying monthly bills.

Figure 2.9 Problems and Opportunities Map.

Describe Future Tasks

Up to this point, your analysis activity has been aimed at understanding and documenting the users and their current work. Now, however, it is time to start focusing on the future. At this point you should gather everything you have so far about the users, the project, the constraints, the results of your task analysis, and the problems and opportunities map. You are ready to create new task flows that describe the future.

One thing you will have to decide up front is how much of your future task description is going to be an ideal world scenario, and how much is going to conform to given constraints. You should decide this point of view before you describe the future tasks so that you will not spend time on systems that cannot be implemented.

Describing the future tasks is similar to documenting current tasks. The best tools for describing future tasks are similar to some of the ones you used to describe current tasks. Task charts or task sketches can both be useful. Usually we do not use task detail tables to describe future tasks—by the time we are ready for that level of detail about the future we are ready to move on to use case scenarios (described below).

Figure 2.10 shows part of the future Task Sketch for the Check-Ease Paying Bills task.

How does documenting current and future tasks differ from business process reengineering? Business process reengineering (BPR) makes decisions about how the business will operate, for example, how an order will move through from inception to fulfillment. BPR often fails to take these decisions through to the level of how an individual or group of people in a certain job will carry out specific tasks. Task analysis takes BPR into account, but goes into more detail in describing exactly how users will do their work. If BPR is happening on your project, you will want to have all possible data and decisions from the BPR group before and during your task analysis work.

Develop Usability Specifications

Once you have analyzed current and future tasks, you are ready to specify what you mean by usable or user-friendly for this interface.

Figure 2.10 Part of the future Task Sketch for Paying Bills with Check-Ease.

These are your usability specifications. Usability specifications provide a powerful means for pinning down and communicating what usability, ease of use, and user-friendly really mean for a system and its interface. For example, for a given project, is it more important that the interface provide ease of learning or ease of use? How important is it that the new interface be compatible with the user interface that the users are familiar with now? Usability specifications summarize key user, training, and documentation assumptions in a format that is objective, measurable, and testable.

Usability specifications should be defined at the start of every project. If you can't clearly define what user-friendly means for the system, how will you know when you have achieved it? And how will you prioritize feature and interface design work?

Usability specifications can also provide a typically much needed common vision for the new system. When there are heated arguments about an interface design among project participants, often, underlying these arguments, are very different visions of the usability goals for the system. For example, marketing is concerned because informal testing shows users can't immediately perform some complex task using the system (usability goal = walk-up-and-use), but the interface designers assumed users would be trained and use the product all day, every day (usability goal = flexibility).

To develop usability specifications, first identify three to ten key usability attributes for the system. Consult with project management, marketing, and users to identify these attributes. Examples of usability attributes are:

❑ Ease of learning

❑ Rapid task performance

❑ Accurate task performance

❑ Perceived ease of use

Good questions to ask when looking for key usability attributes are: What problems is the new user interface supposed to solve? Is the interface suppose to improve speed or accuracy of user performance on key tasks? Or to reduce required time to train users? Or to improve user evaluations of system ease of use?

Once you have identified usability attributes, you can develop usability specifications. The three steps in developing specifications are detailed below.

1. For each usability attribute, identify how the interface could be measured on that attribute. Examples of usability measures are:

   ❑ Time to train to a performance criterion
   ❑ Time to complete a task
   ❑ Number of errors in completing a task
   ❑ Percentage of users that successfully complete the task
   ❑ Time to relearn to criterion
   ❑ Time spent correcting errors
   ❑ Average ease-of-use rating given by users surveyed/interviewed

2. For each usability measure, specify what constitutes success. For example:

   ❑ 20 minutes
   ❑ Two errors
   ❑ Fifty percent rate 8 or better on scale of 10

   You may want to specify criteria for both the minimum acceptable level of usability and for the target level of usability.

   Good places to look for usability criteria: What is clearly unacceptable performance? What is current performance that must be improved upon? How does the competition perform? Be careful not to select unrealistic usability performance criteria; for example, "One hundred percent of users can perform task A with 100% accuracy." Usability specifications are a tool to clarify real project goals and measure real system performance.

3. Include other key elements.

   ❑ Make sure that the usability goals that are written include all assumptions about who users will be (user profiles) and how much preexisting knowledge and training they will be expected to have.
   ❑ Be sure to get the participation of project management, development, training, and documentation in writing and reviewing usability goals.

Figure 2.11 shows some usability specifications for the Check-Ease interface.

Another way to document usability specifications is in a usability specifications table. Figure 2.12 shows a sample table for the Check-Ease application. The specifications still have the same components. If you are not familiar with writing usability specifications, this format may be useful.

Usability Specifications for Check-Ease

Ease of Learning

With no previous training and using only online help and documentation, 90% of adults who read and write English, currently have a checking account and currently use other MS Windows applications, can start the Check-Ease application, open a sample checkbook, and record a check in less than 15 minutes the first time.

Ease of Use

After having correctly started the Check-Ease application and recorded a check at least three times, 75% of adult users can do this task in five minutes or less (IBM 386 PC or PC clone).

Ease of Learning

After completing a short (20 minutes or less) tutorial, and using online help and documentation, 75% of adults who currently have a checking account, do or do not balance their checkbook, currently use other MS Windows applications, and read and write English can correctly balance a sample checkbook.

Ease of Learning

Seventy-five percent of adult IBM PC (or clone) users with MS Windows experience and who read and write English can successfully set up the Check-Ease modem features in 20 minutes or less. Ninety percent can do this in 40 minutes or less.

Ease of Learning

After a 20-minute tutorial, and using only online help and documentation, 90% of adults who read and write English, currently have a checking account and currently use other MS Windows applications, can pay bills in less than 30 minutes the first time.

Figure 2.11 Usability Specifications Narrative for Check-Ease.

Measurable Behavior	Criteria	Key Elements	Users
Pay 10 bills	Within 30 minutes the first time and 20 minutes subsequent times	Online help and 20-minute tutorial are available, and tutorial is used	Read English, use Windows, have an account

Figure 2.12 Usability Specifications Table for Check-Ease.

Develop Use Case Scenarios

A use case scenario is an outline of tasks and subtasks that describes how users will do their work. The purpose of the use case scenario is to aid in conceptual design. It must describe how users will do their work with the new software so that the correct flow of screens can be developed.

How is a use case scenario different from future task descriptions? Parts of the future task description assume a new software solution, but not necessarily all of the future tasks involve an interface. Scenarios detail only the tasks that involve the interface you are going to design. They are the link between the future task description and the design of the interface.

The use case scenario is not a reengineering document, though it may reflect reengineered processes. The use case scenario describes how the users will do their work when the new software is in place—not how the work is done now, or what the problems are with how it's done now. Another major difference between business process reengineering documents and use case scenarios is that use case scenarios document users' tasks. Business process reengineering documents usually describe a business process, for example, how an order moves through the department, and don't necessarily describe it from the user's point of view.

Sample use case scenario for our Check-Ease system is shown in Figure 2.13.

To create effective scenarios, follow these guidelines:

❑ *Write from the user's point of view, not the system's point of view.* In order to match the way the users should be doing their work,

---

Use Case Scenario:

Paying Bills with Printed Checks

1. Enter bills (payee name and amount due) on a worksheet.

2. View the new balance (current balance less each payment amount).

3. Decide if there are enough funds to pay the bills.

   a. If yes (80% of the time), go to step 4.

   b. If no (20% of the time), mark the bills not to be paid (80%) or change payment amounts (20%), then go to step 4.

4. Tell system to pay the bills.

5. Set printing options for checks.

6. Put check stock in printer.

7. Print checks.

8. Look at checks.

9. Reprint checks if there is a problem (problem with checks 30% of the time).

10. View updated checking account register (viewed 50% of the time).

11. Run reports (50% of the time). Note: see separate scenario for detail on running reports.

Figure 2.13 Use Case Scenario for Paying Bills using Check-Ease.

the scenario must be a list of user tasks. There is a tendency to start to describe what the system is going to do. If you really want a system description in your scenario, create a parallel scenario for the system. Start first with the user's tasks and when the scenario is complete, go back and write what the system is doing at each step.

❑ *Make sure you start with the user's tasks.* In order to be able to use the scenario to create a conceptual model and interface screens you must have a listing of user tasks.

❑ *Include frequency information.* In order to create the best flow of screens later on you must document information on frequency of tasks in the scenario. If there are alternative paths or tasks, or decision points, you need to decide how frequently each path is likely to be taken. Will users be processing a new order most of the time or working with an existing order? This frequency information is critical if the scenario is to be effective. What users do most should be the easiest to do. Your design decisions and tradeoffs come in large measure from this frequency information. For example, if your scenario indicates that working with an existing order occurs 80% of the time, then during design you should start the screen flow for that task with a list of existing orders. If however, your scenario indicates that starting a new order occurs 80% of the time, you should start the screen flow for that task with a blank order, ready to be filled in.

❑ *Make note of exceptions.* If you are documenting frequency, then you will know as you go along which parts of the scenario are describing exceptions. Exceptions should be noted, and eventually need to be filled in, but make sure you have described all the common, frequent, and critical paths before going back to document exceptions.

❑ *Make note of critical tasks.* Some tasks are frequent. Some are infrequent. But another aspect of tasks is criticality. It is possible to have a task that is infrequent, but critical. All critical tasks should be noted on the scenario, especially those that are infrequent, but critical.

❑ *Write in words, not just diagrams.* Diagramming tasks can be powerful, but if you are not familiar with the notation or abbreviations they can be hard to understand. It is very important that everyone on the scenario team be able to read and understand the scenario once it is completed. Also important is that people *not* on the scenario team be able to easily read and understand the scenario. If a person has the correct content matter expertise, he or she should be able to read your scenario without much interpretation. This means the scenario will be more clear and easily understood if it is written using words rather than notations. If you insist on using notation, you should also prepare a version with words only in outline form.

❑ *Describe the future.* A scenario does not describe the user's tasks now, but the tasks they will perform when the new system is in place. It is easy when creating a scenario to fall into describing the current situation, but avoid doing that unless the new is exactly the same as the current. You should instead be documenting in detail how the user will work with the new system.

Interface Scenarios Versus Other Forms of Use Case Scenarios

Use case scenarios are discussed a lot recently because of the use of the term in object-oriented programming methodologies by Ivar Jacobson and others. In some ways we are using the term in the same way as it is used within a development methodology, and in other ways we have modified the definition.

Use case scenarios for interface design need to be focused on the user's actions as they interact with the new software. Use case scenarios as we have seen them used by development groups sometimes contain this information, but it is often woven into a description of what the software is doing behind the scenes. Figure 2.14 shows an example of a scenario written from a systems point of view.

The description of software actions is critical for software developers, but is at best a distraction for interface designers, and at worst, can cause new interface designers to veer away from true interface design, and move inappropriately into designing the underlying software.

It is reasonable, perhaps critical, that both interface designers and the software development group be working from the same use case

---

System Scenario

The user enters each bill (payee name and amount) into the system. The system shows a running balance, starting with the current balance, less the amount of each bill as it is entered. The user can deselect a bill or change the amount to be paid. The system recalculates as changes are made. When the bills are processed for payment, the system prints out the checks, updates the checking account register, and recalculates the balance.

Figure 2.14 System Scenario.

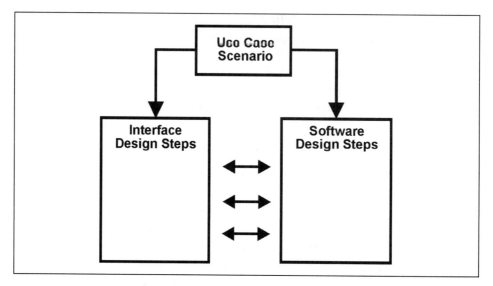

Figure 2.15 Shared Use Case Scenario.

scenario. Figure 2.15 shows how both interface design and software design could come from a common scenario.

To ensure that both sides have a usable scenario, you could create two separate, but matching scenarios, one for the user actions and one for system activities. That way, both groups (interface designers and developers) are getting the same scenario, but each group can get the information it needs. Each group also has the advantage of seeing (if desired) what the other group is working from. Figure 2.16 shows an example of separate but matching scenarios.

Another approach is to first create the interface design version and then have the software group add what they need for the software development side. What is important is that those responsible for the next phase of interface design have a version to work from that has what they need (user tasks from the user's point of view), and that if the development team is also using scenarios, that the scenarios cover the same actions.

Holding Use Case Scenario Sessions

Before you create use case scenarios, the major business decisions need to be made. You don't want to be discussing business decisions

Use Case Scenario: **Paying Bills with Printed Checks**	System Scenario: **Paying Bills with Printed Checks**
1. Enter bills (payee name and amount due) on a worksheet.	1. System shows data for each bill: payee, due date, and amount due; system shows current balance in checking account.
2. View the new balance (current balance less each payment amount).	2. System recalculates the balance as each bill is entered, if the bill is to be paid.

3. Decide if there are enough funds to pay the bills.
  a. If yes (80% of the time), go to step 4.
  b. If no (20% of the time), mark the bills not to be paid (80%) or change payment amounts (20%), then go to step 4.
	3. Show changed amount if user changes amount to pay. Mark as unselected if user chooses not to pay a bill.

4. Tell system to pay the bills.	4. System enters bill as an entry in the checking account register and recalculates the current balance.
5. Set printing options for checks.	5. Displays options for printing checks.
6. Put check stock in printer.	6. None.
7. Print checks.	7. System prints checks.
8. Look at checks.	8. None.
9. Reprint checks if there is a problem (problem with checks 30% of the time).	9. Alert user about printing status. Allow user to enter which checks to reprint if necessary.
10. View updated checking account register (viewed 50% of the time).	10. Show updated checking account register.
11. Run reports (50% of the time). Note: see separate scenario for detail on running reports.	11. See separate scenario for running reports.

Figure 2.16 Separated Scenario.

during the use case scenario sessions, because this will slow you down, and the people able to discuss and decide on those issues may not be present. Discussions on such things as the new software's scope and performance should have occurred while documenting current and future tasks. Items that have not been discussed or decided upon will have to be dealt with before you can continue with your use case scenarios.

If you have not documented the tasks, your use case scenario sessions will be slow and difficult, because you will have to do the documenting of current and future tasks as you go along. Below are tips for running a useful and efficient session.

❑ *Remember the definition of a use case scenario.* Stay focused on the future and don't lapse into describing how the work is done now. Document the user's actions, not what the system is doing.

❑ *Keep in mind the level of detail you need.* You need enough detail to sketch screens later, but you don't need to decide exactly how many characters are in the name field.

❑ *Know where to start and what to include.* Document the most important and frequent tasks first. Make sure you capture the frequency and criticality of each task.

❑ *Pay attention to the environment.* Make sure you have enough white boards. Meet in a comfortable room with good lighting, ventilation, and noise control. Pick a place where people won't be interrupted or called away.

❑ *Give the team two to four hours per session.* Less than that, you can't accomplish enough. More than that, everyone gets too tired.

❑ *Make sure everyone wants to be there.* Having someone on the team that doesn't want to participate will make it difficult on the rest of the team and will slow you down.

❑ *Be willing to give the facilitator power.* The facilitator's job is difficult. Everyone on the team must be willing to be guided.

❑ *Keep track of questions that arise and need clarification or answers.* Decide before the session ends who is responsible for getting answers to the questions.

You will need members of your team to take the following roles:

1. *Facilitator.* The facilitator is a critical role. The facilitator keeps the group on track. The facilitator needs to be impartial: no hidden agendas, just a desire to accurately capture in detail what the user tasks are, and what they should be on the new system. Critical facilitator skills and actions include:

❑ Knowing when to keep asking questions versus when to just write something down and come back to it later

❑ Writing down enough detail to capture the information, but not so much as to slow down the process

❑ Being willing to erase and redo as new information emerges

❑ Knowing when to put something on an "issues to be resolved" list and move on

❑ Making sure everyone is participating

❑ Making sure that the group stays focused on capturing information and not sketching screens

❑ Not letting any one person dominate conversations

❑ Knowing when the group is tired and needs a break

❑ Knowing when a particular task is done and it is time to work on another

If someone on the team is experienced at group facilitation, you may want to pick that person for this role. The interface designer can be the facilitator. *Content experts/users should not facilitate.* The content experts/users need to be free to think and do not have time to facilitate. The facilitator does not need to be a content expert. Familiarity with the subject matter helps, in order to ask meaningful questions, but it is often better that the facilitator not be an expert, since lack of knowledge can lead to some good questions.

2. *Scribe.* Someone should be assigned the job of making sure the work gets captured and documented when complete. When the team agrees they are done with one task, the scribe should record the task so that the board can be erased for the next one.

3. *Other members.* The role of other members in the group is to listen and ask questions and clarify. Technical people or interface designers are not the source of main information during analysis. They are there to listen, ask questions, clarify, and experience the discussions.

Test

The results from the Analysis phase are critical—they are the basis for the next phase where actual screens, dialog boxes, menus, and win-

Analysis Checklist	
✔	*Step*
	Identify current state and scope
	Consider work in progress
	Decide on the scope of the analysis
	Define interface design constraints
	Develop user profiles
	Gather data
	Validate user profiles
	Gather task data
	Document the current tasks
	Decide how to document the current tasks
	Document current tasks
	Validate current task documents
	Document problems and opportunities
	Document problems and opportunities
	Validate problems and opportunities
	Describe future tasks
	Describe future tasks
	Validate future task descriptions
	Develop usability specifications
	Develop specifications
	Validate specifications
	Develop use case scenarios
	Develop use case scenarios
	Validate use case scenarios

Figure 2.17 Analysis Checklist.

dows are created. Therefore, it is important that you test and verify the decisions you make during analysis.

There are many test activities that go on during the Analysis phase:

❑ The user profiles need to be validated by either going into the field and making sure they are accurate portrayals, and/or showing them to users and their managers for verification.

❑ It is critical that current and future task descriptions be verified with users, their managers, and any other key stakeholders.

❑ Usability specifications need to be verified and agreed to by users, their managers, and key stakeholders.

❑ Use case scenarios need to be verified with users, and their managers. If the software developers are using scenarios for their architecture design, then they need to verify and agree to the scenarios as well.

You may want each of these tests or verifications to be a formal step with sign-offs. If so, you will need to determine exactly who should be signing off on each one—it might vary slightly, for example, while the software developers might be helped by seeing user profiles, the use case scenarios are critical to their work.

Summary

Analysis ensures that your interface design decisions fit the users and their work. Figure 2.17 is a checklist to follow when performing analysis.

Design

Analysis	Design	Construction
Identify Scope Develop User Profiles Gather Data Document Current Tasks Document Opportunities Describe Future Tasks Develop Usability Specs Develop Scenarios Test	**Choose Objects** **Select Metaphors** **Storyboard** **Create High Level Design** **Test** **Develop Support Plan**	Develop Prototype Test Prototype Document the Design

Contents

Purpose

Deliverables

Preparation

Process

Summary

Designing usable interfaces is both a science and an art, and it is during the Design phase that science and art are evident. During this phase you take everything you have learned during analysis and create a solution based on all that you know. The steps in this phase are a combination of designing interface models and metaphors, deciding on overall appearance and organization, and storyboarding and documenting your design with paper mockups.

Purpose

The purpose of this phase is to consciously create a conceptual model for the interface. In creating the conceptual model, you are deliberately creating a model for the screen world where users will perform the tasks the system is to cover. You then translate that model into appearance and organization—a high level design. By following the steps below, you ensure that you have used all of the information you have available from analysis, and that you are applying that information to create a good design. In the next phase, Construction, you will prototype your design.

At the end of the Design phase, you have mockups of screens that:

❑ Portray all major/frequent/critical tasks

❑ Make major user objects obvious

❑ Have clear and usable metaphors

❑ Match the way the users need to work as described in the use case scenarios

❑ Contain enough detail to be able to walk through the interface with others not involved in creating the design

Deliverables

When you have completed the interface design phase you have the following deliverables:

❑ *Object-attribute-action table.* User objects with the attributes that describe them and the actions performed on them.

- ❑ *Object-metaphor-representations table.* Possible metaphors and how to represent them.
- ❑ *Storyboards of objects and metaphors.* Drawings of how objects and metaphors would look on screens.
- ❑ *Action table.* Summary of all actions and decisions about how users will take them (menus, buttons, and so on.).
- ❑ *High-level design mockups.* Paper prototypes of all main windows and screens to use to show your design to others and get feedback.
- ❑ *Support plan.* Preliminary training and documentation plans for the interface.

Preparation

Before you begin interface design you need to gather all the results from the analysis phase, create a team for interface design, disseminate the materials from analysis, and prepare a place to work together.

The Design Team

Design is a team effort. Because it is a creative, brainstorming, iterative process, it requires the input of more than one person. Think ahead about the interdisciplinary nature of your team. Your team should consist of three to six people. A team of more than six people finds it hard to work together and make decisions.

The interface design team should be similar to, but does not have to be exactly the same as, the analysis team. During Analysis the focus was on content domain. During interface Design the focus is on interface issues. Some of the team members will be the same, and should be the same. Do not hand off interface design to an entirely different set of people. On the other hand, you may want to consider some new members as described below:

- ❑ *One or two interface designers.* The interface designers will know how to best translate the user's tasks as described in the use case scenarios into major user objects, metaphors, and a flow of screens with controls.

- ❑ *One or two users.* Even if you are working from a use case scenario, many questions will arise about how the work should really be done while you are modeling. You still need a content expert while you are creating the model.
- ❑ *A technical person.* Involving a technical person is critical at this juncture. You want to make sure that the model you create is actually implementable within the technical (software and hardware) constraints you have.

Other people you may want on your team include:

- ❑ *A graphic designer.* A graphic designer can sketch your ideas quickly as you talk, especially when you are discussing metaphors. This can be a valuable addition to the process.
- ❑ *A training/support/documentation specialist.* Someone in training, support, or documentation will always have ease of use and learning in mind, and would also appreciate knowing early what direction you are heading towards.

Design Sessions

When the team meets to work on interface design, prepare a room with enough space to move around. Make sure you have large white boards so that everyone can see what is going on. Designing is a democratic process—everyone needs to have the ability to pick up a pen and start sketching or writing.

Each session should be at least two hours, preferably four hours at a time if possible. It takes a while to get the creative juices flowing, and you don't want to have to stop just as you get rolling.

Before you start designing you need to have a use case scenario completed for the portion of the interface you are ready to model. This prerequisite is critical. If you don't have a use case scenario ready, you will spend all of your time trying to create one. Try to have all unresolved issues from the scenario sessions answered before you start designing.

If you have several use case scenarios for the interface you are designing, it is best to start with a scenario that represents a frequent and/or critical task. You want the model of the whole interface to be based around these frequent and critical tasks.

A natural tendency is to design the high-level menu, launching pad, or beginning tasks first. Don't start with the menu bar, launching pad, or highest-level task. Until you have created a conceptual model and have sketches for a number of different tasks, you will not know how they should fit together, whether they should share a menu, and so on.

Process

A conceptual model is the plan or blueprint for how the user will *see* the interface. It is a model of the interface, not of the underlying software structure. In order for users to be able to predict what will happen next, and make decisions about what they should do next, they need to have a mental model of how the software works. A conceptual model conveys to users a working model of the interface.

Software designers often jump immediately from existing or proposed system design to detailed interface design, translating the software professional's view of the system (and jargon) into a set of windows populated with GUI objects (pull-down menus, command buttons, scroll bars, and so on.). The result is a set of interface windows and dialog boxes that should promote ease of learning and use, but users are as lost and confused when using the new GUI as they were with its non-GUI predecessors. Because the interface is a direct translation of the system model, users can't form a good mental model of how the system works and how they should interact with the interface to accomplish their goals. They describe the interface as "unfriendly."

Design is the critical step that identifies the user objects, actions, and metaphors that should be portrayed (represented) in the interface so that users can understand the interface and learn to use it effectively to accomplish their goals. The translation of this conceptual design into graphical user interface objects (for example, windows, command buttons, and so on.) is accomplished later in this interface design phase when you create a design mockup, and during the construction phase when you develop a computer or hi-fi prototype. Figure 3.1 illustrates that user objects are not the same as interface widgets.

User Objects	GUI Objects (Widgets)
Trash Can	Windows
Checkbook	Menus
Form	Boxes
Calculator	Controls
Document	Icons
Paragraph	Cursors

Figure 3.1 User objects are not the same as GUI widgets.

The interface design phase has several steps:

❑ Choose major user objects.
❑ Select metaphors and representations.
❑ Storyboard the objects and metaphors.
❑ Create a high level interface design.
❑ Test.
❑ Describe the support plan.

Choose Major User Objects

Major user objects are the things in your interface that users have to manipulate, either literally or figuratively, as they move through their work flow. These interface objects are usually related to, but not necessarily the same as underlying software objects, or the objects described in object-oriented analysis and design. Interface objects are objects in the representational world that you are creating with the interface.

Major user object design involves making conscious decisions about these objects. Careful consideration needs to be given to the possible objects that users could manipulate during a particular task. Not all objects that users might interact with should be major user objects. It is critical that the interface design team decide which objects are the most important so that the design can be built around them. Interfaces without clear and obvious user objects are hard to design and hard to learn and use.

The steps to follow when choosing major user objects are described below.

Identify Objects from Analysis Documents

Use the information gathered from site visits and observing and interviewing targeted users in the Analysis phase to identify the objects users will want to see and act on in the interface when performing the tasks the system supports. For example, do users talk about *clients, projects, employees*? Are their tasks "create a *new budget*," "update an *employee list*"? What did you see them manipulate when they performed their tasks, for example, *schedules, worksheets, lists, plans, reports*? These are the objects the interface needs to portray.

One of the most concentrated places to examine potential major user objects is in the use case scenarios. Look for the things (nouns, objects) that the user has to manipulate or take actions on (view, edit, enter). Figure 3.2 shows the use case scenario for paying monthly bills with objects marked.

Make a list of all the possible major user objects you have identified. Then examine the list and eliminate any objects that users don't really need to see or take action on in the interface to do the tasks they care about. These are internal, software objects, and they can be implicit—the software developers will need to know about them, but they do not need to explicitly appear in your interface, nor does the entire interface need to be built around them.

If you look closely at your list of candidates for major user objects, you will probably identify some objects that are sub-objects of other objects. For example, the object "list of awards and promotions" might really be a sub-object of "employee file." The object "slide" might be a sub-object of the object "slide presentation."

Figure 3.3 shows part of the Object-Action Table for the Check-Ease application. Notice that some objects have been identified as sub-objects. They are indented in the left column.

Identify Object Attributes

Next, identify key object attributes, that is, the information about the objects that users need to see when performing tasks. For example: the

---

Use Case Scenario: Paying Bills

---

1. Enter bills (payee name and amount due) on a worksheet.

2. View the new balance (current balance less each payment amount).

3. Decide if there are enough funds to pay the bills.

   a. If yes (80% of the time), go to step 4.

   b. If no (20% of the time), mark the bills not to be paid (80%) or change payment amounts (20%), then go to step 4.

4. Tell system to pay the bills.

5. Set printing options for checks.

6. Put check stock in printer.

7. Print checks.

8. Look at checks.

9. Reprint checks if there is a problem (problem with checks 30% of the time).

10. View updated checking account register (viewed 50% of the time).

11. Run reports (50% of the time). Note: see separate scenario for detail on running reports.

Figure 3.2 Use Case Scenario for Paying Bills using Check-Ease with user objects highlighted.

day, time, and purpose of an appointment; the name, social security number, and department of an employee; the date, number, amount, and payee of a check, are object attributes. The middle column in Figure 3.3 shows the attributes for some Check-Ease user objects.

Identify User Actions on Task Objects

Using information in your task analyses and use case scenarios, identify needed user (not system) actions on each of the objects and sub-

Object/Sub-Object	Attributes	User Actions
Checkbook	Bank name or other checkbook name (e.g., Personal, Business) Account number Start date End date	Start a new checkbook Name Delete Print
Checkbook register	Checkbook entries Running balance	View Navigate Add entry Print Sort
Checkbook entry	Type (e.g., Deposit, Withdrawal, ATM, etc.) Amount Date Cleared/not cleared Note	View Edit Copy and Paste Print Void Find Move
Running balance	Value	View Adjust
Blank check	Checkbook/account number User entries (amount, payee, etc.)	View Write/Edit Copy Print Send/Transfer
Telephone transfer	Type (e.g., Payment, Account Transfer, etc.) Status (e.g., completed, in progress) Date Amount etc.	View Create Start Stop etc.
etc.		

Figure 3.3 Part of the Object-Action Table for Check-Ease.

Object/Sub-Objects	Attributes	User Actions
Bills Worksheet	Date created/saved	Start
		Save/Name
		View
		Navigate
		Print
Bill	Payee name	Enter a bill
	Amount due	Change amount
	Amount to pay	Delete
		Pay

Figure 3.4 More of the Object-Action Table for Check-Ease.

objects. Identify the terminology users use when describing these actions. For example, do users talk about *filing* and *copying* a file? Do they talk about *changing* and *moving* an appointment? Do they say they *review* and *distribute* a report? These actions are in the last column in the Object-Action Table (Figure 3.3).

Figure 3.4 shows two more objects for the Check-Ease application.

Once you have decided on major user objects, you want to make sure that those objects are obvious and clear to the user as you design your interface. You will do this in subsequent steps as you decide on metaphors and create design mockups.

Select Metaphors and Representations

Metaphors are the tools we use to link highly technical, complex software with the users' everyday world. They are visual and conceptual representations of major user objects and their associated actions. For example, using a list as a metaphor implies that the user will see a vertical array of information (the list) and that they will be able to take certain expected actions (add something to the list or delete something from it). The list might look a lot like a paper list that the user uses currently, in which case the metaphor is a visual representation. Sometimes, however, you may not be able to visually represent the metaphor in detail. Calling something a rolodex does not mean that it has to visually and physically resemble a rolodex. It might be enough that you call it a rolodex, that it contain name and address information, and that it be organized alphabetically. This representation would be conceptual rather than visual. It is still using a metaphor.

A metaphor may be helpful when part or all of the interface involves functions or features that are new to the targeted users. A good metaphor can help users connect what they don't know with what they do know. The desktop metaphor seen in the Apple Macintosh interface and the IBM Presentation Manager office metaphor are good examples: Common office objects (desk, file, folder, in box) are used in the interface instead of their more unfamiliar system counterparts (directories, operating system functions, and so on.).

Sometimes designers say they decided not to use a metaphor in a particular interface. It could be argued, however, that there is *always* a metaphor operating; whether the designer has chosen one consciously or not, there is a metaphor. A common metaphor in GUI applications is the form. Screens look like data on a paper form. A form might be a good metaphor for your application, or it might be a very poor one. If you do not choose a metaphor consciously, you will probably end up with some kind of form. But is it the right form? The best form? Would a list or spreadsheet have been better than a form? It is better spending time deciding what the metaphor is or should be rather than ending up with one by default. Below are some guidelines for choosing effective metaphors:

❑ *Make sure your metaphor holds up to users' primary assumptions.* As shown in Figure 3.5, when users notice that the screen they are using is like a rolodex card, they will make assumptions about functionality and interaction. They will assume that they can move through the file alphabetically. They will assume they can add or change information.

❑ *The metaphor does not have to be a full visual representation.* Labeling a screen as a worksheet is effective even if it doesn't look exactly like a paper worksheet.

❑ *The best metaphors are simple.* They do not have to be unique.

❑ *Look to the users' physical world.* One of the best places to find good metaphors is the users' task world—the objects they use now in performing their work, for example, report, notepad, appointment book, plan, ledger, and so on. However, don't be bound by these. The lousy form they've been using in hard copy may not be the best metaphor to put online. Get feedback from users on possible metaphors.

❑ *More than one is OK.* As a matter of fact, more than one metaphor is probably required. For example, users may need to first fill out a *worksheet* and then run a *report*.

❑ *Reflect major user objects.* Make sure the major user objects you chose are well represented by the metaphor. Metaphors include both object and actions taken upon the object. For instance, using a rolodex as a metaphor implies the use of cards as an object, as well as actions such as moving forward and backward alphabetically.

❑ *A metaphor should be conscious to the designer.* However, users may not consciously recognize it or be able to articulate it. This is okay. A metaphor does not have to be conscious to the user for it to be effective.

Figure 3.5 Users make assumptions about metaphors.

After you have chosen a metaphor for each of your major user objects, you will want to explore ideas for representing the objects in the interface. One of the most powerful features of a GUI is that the objects and actions of interest to the user are visually portrayed. Unlike the "black box" dialogs of older, character-based terminal interfaces, users can see the information they manipulate and can see the results of their actions on this information. Often graphical portrayal of this information makes these interface objects look very much like their physical, real world counterparts; for example, an interface spreadsheet has lined rows and columns just like its paper equivalent, an electronic mail in box looks like a miniature version of its plastic or metal equivalent.

Don't get caught up at this point, however, in detailed design. For example, at this point in the process it's enough to know that a spreadsheet object might best be represented by an accountant-style grid; it's too soon to spend time on designing the grid and a window that might contain it.

Don't get caught up in trying to represent all objects pictorially, either. Sometimes, a picture is *not* better than words, and an alphanumeric representation is the best way to portray an object (and can be an important way to save screen space). For example, an alphanumeric list of employees would usually be a better way to represent a department than would a pictorial representation of a floor in an office building with little desks. (It would depend on the users' task, for example, find an employee's name versus find an employee's desk.)

Deciding on metaphors and representations is different from the object or entity analyses performed when designing the data base for the system. The elements may be very similar, but it is critical to remember that the goal here is to identify those objects that users need to see and act on in the interface and how they will be viewed by users, not the database objects, programming objects, or graphical widgets that will be used for their implementation. For example, users may see an important difference between a report and a memo and want to see both objects in their interface world, while these may be represented by the same object (text file) in the system. Also, the source for identifying these objects is analysis of user tasks and terminology, not a logical analysis.

Object/Sub-Object	Metaphors	Representations
Bills worksheet	Worksheet	"Balance Sheet" 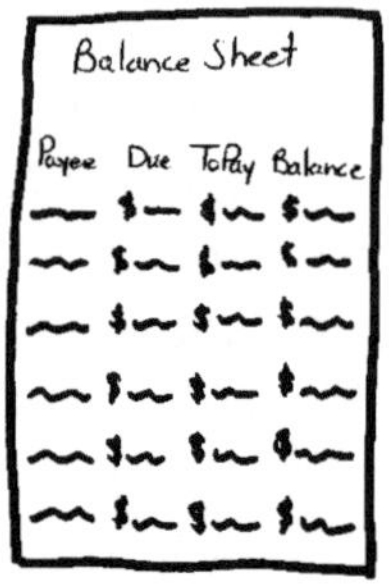 or "Spread Sheet" 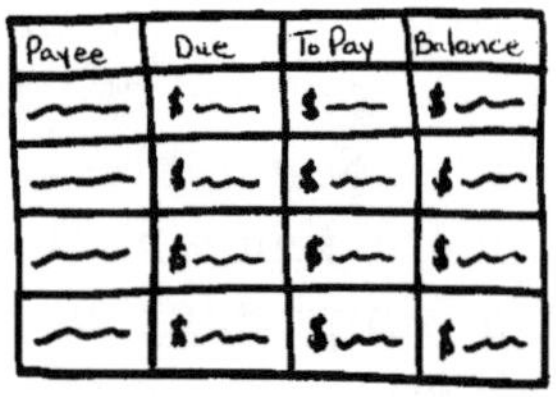

Figure 3.6 Part of the Object-Metaphor-Representations Table for Check-Ease.

You can summarize your ideas about metaphors and representations in an Object-Metaphor-Representations table. Figure 3.6 shows part of the Object-Metaphor-Representations table for Check-Ease.

Storyboard the Major User Objects and Metaphors

While developing your conceptual model, sketch out your object, action, metaphor, and representation ideas. Quickly storyboard your decisions with pencil and paper or on a dry-erase board. This allows you to visually see the result of the decisions you are making. For example,

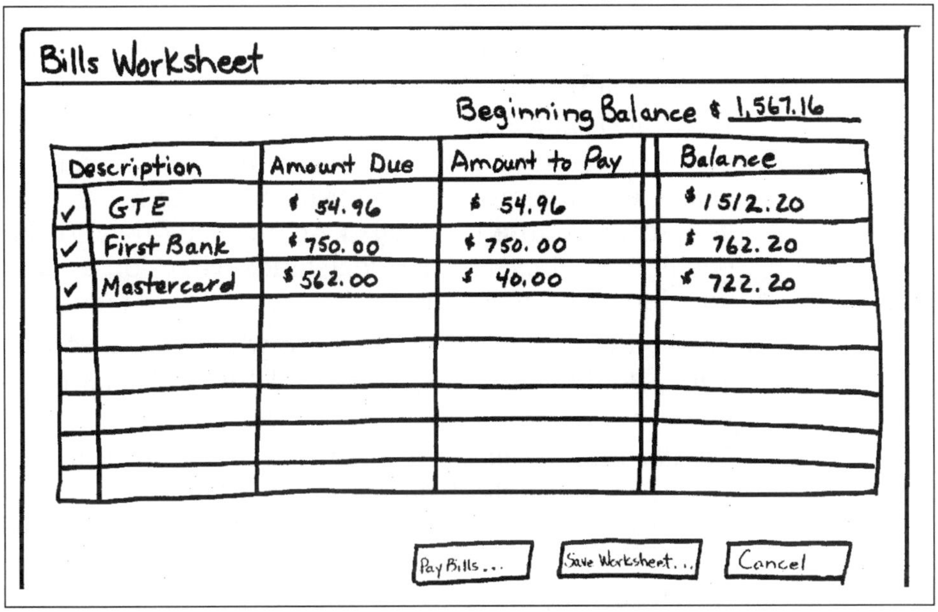

Figure 3.7 Storyboard of Check-Ease Bills Worksheet.

objects can be portrayed as text, tables or pictures. Users may need multiple representations or views of the same object, for example, a text view and a map view of a delivery schedule.

This is a good time to adjust the model or the representation of it. Take a use case scenario for one of the major tasks in the interface. Apply your objects, actions, and metaphors and representations to the scenario. Sketch out some screens and windows using your decisions and the scenario. Does it work? Do you want to modify any of the object or metaphor decisions? This storyboard is not an entire mockup of your interface, but just some preliminary sketches. Figure 3.7 is a storyboard of our Bills Worksheet.

Here are some points to remember about storyboarding:

❑ *Sketch on an erasable medium.* Storyboards need to be rough, because there are a lot of critical design decisions you make as you storyboard and you need the freedom to quickly erase and redo during the process. For this reason you should storyboard on paper or white boards, not on computer. Trying to do storyboarding on a computer screen without first working on paper is a major interface design mistake. We like to use small (8 ½ x 11) static paper that acts like a portable dry-erase board (it sticks on any wall).

❑ _Keep storyboards rough._ If you put in too much time and detail on each screen you will not be willing to erase and start again. Intelligent interface design means building in iterations. Find a good compromise between sketching roughly and sketching in detail, so that everyone understands what you are drawing but you don't get slowed down.

❑ _Involve users._ Make sure users are with you as you storyboard. They should be an integral part of the decisions that are being made.

❑ _Consult a technical person._ Make sure a technical person is involved or available if needed—you want to make sure you are not creating an interface that is impossible to implement.

❑ _Storyboard common flow first._ When you begin storyboarding, storyboard the most frequently used tasks. This is called storyboarding common paths. The scenarios you are storyboarding from should have the tasks and subtasks with their frequency. Tasks with high frequency are common path. Tasks with low frequency are exceptions. You want to first sketch a series of screens that matches the common path. If you deal with the exceptions the first time through you will get stuck, waste time, and build a model around exceptions. You will be able to build in exceptions later, during high-level interface design. Your first time through, concentrate on the common paths.

This process of deciding on major user objects, actions, metaphors, representations, and storyboarding should be completed for each major use case scenario you developed. After you have these conceptual designs for each scenario, you are ready to put it all together into a high level interface design.

Create a High Level Interface Design

Once you have made object, metaphor, and representation decisions, and have storyboarded your scenarios, you are ready to create a high-level design for the interface. We realize this is counter to how many designers want to work—they want to create a high-level design of the menus, toolbars, opening windows, and so on, before they have sketched out any storyboards at the scenario level. But how can you know what the high-level design looks like unless you have made some object-metaphor-representation decisions first?

In this step of Design, you:

❑ Select/adapt a style.

❑ Identify main windows and related user actions.

❑ Identify home bases and launching pads.

❑ Identify how users access main windows.

❑ Assign user actions for main windows.

❑ Create design mockups.

Each of these steps is described below.

Select/Adapt a Style

Interface standards and guidelines define how interface components like windows, menus, command buttons, scroll bars, and so on should appear (look) and behave (feel) in the interface. They provide designers with guidance for detailed interface design aspects such as window and menu layout, interaction techniques such as selection and direct manipulation, and use of mouse buttons and keyboard commands. Conformance to a standard style encourages the development of a consistent interface.

Often, compliance with a vendor's standard style such as IBM's Common User Access (CUA), the Macintosh style, or Microsoft's Windows will already have been identified as one of the project's requirements from the start. If not, an interface standard style should be selected or developed to provide a consistent look and feel for the user interface.

However, standard vendor interface styles still leave much detailed design to the interface designer, such as project-specific icon designs and use of color. Some of these may be covered in enterprise-wide guidelines. Part II of this book provides a starting point for customizing your own enterprise-wide guidelines. Still more specific guidelines for a particular project can be specified and communicated to developers in a project interface style guide once a complete, detailed interface design has been developed, at the end of the Construction phase.

As you begin to decide on windows and screens you may be borrowing or adapting an entire high level design or parts of one. Be careful: very often teams fall into a particular design without realizing. For example, the design team thinks that all the parts of the application have to look and work like the office suite product they use enterprise-wide. They begin to force-fit the particular interface they are designing into a document office suite model. From there they decide that each document must be able to remain open independently, that there can be no buttons on the screens, that they have to use a multiple document interface, and so on. Some of these decisions might be good ones, but many times designers don't make these decisions, they assume them. You must separate out interface guidelines and industry look and feel (for example, we're using Windows 95 look and feel for the Check-Ease interface) from high-level design decisions (everything must work like a separate document). These are two different decisions, and one does not necessarily have to follow from the other. Don't try to force-fit a high-level design model where it doesn't work.

Identify Main Windows and Related User Actions

Intuitive, user-friendly GUIs draw their success with users from more than just the use of icons and command buttons. Their high-level design consists of one, or only a few, main (primary) window(s). These windows represent objects from the users' task world or a good metaphor that the user can understand, such as spreadsheet, employee file, slide presentation, checkbook. Other windows may be displayed in the course of user interaction with these windows (secondary windows), but the main windows provide one or a few recognizable home base(s). Moreover, when working with the object portrayed in the window, users can perform a set of related actions (for example, Print, Save, Copy), and perform them in any order they like.

Identify the main interface windows that will represent the main objects users want to see and act on in the interface in order to achieve their task goals. These objects are the ones you chose as major user objects in the steps above.

Identify Home Bases and Launching Pads

A home base is a screen or window users return to repeatedly while performing a task. A home base contains meaningful information that provides context for the user—where they are and what they're to do next. It might be a list, a form to be completed, or a screen containing status information. It is not, however, a blank screen with a menu bar or logo. You may choose to have several home bases in an application, one for each major task users perform.

Home base is not necessarily the first screen users encounter. For instance, they may go through a series of filters before reaching the list of contracts to be worked on in a particular session. The list of contracts is the real home base.

Many seemingly unrelated complaints can be traced back to the lack of a home base. If you're hearing comments like "There are too many windows," "There are too many keystrokes," or "Can't you fit everything on one screen?" it may be because you've chosen the wrong home base, or have none at all. Users often know when they're feeling "homeless," but are unable to articulate it. Having a home base provides a visual and cognitive anchor. As users perform their work, they return to this anchor again and again, alleviating the feeling of being lost.

A launching pad is a first screen that is used as a jumping-off point for a large application with several smaller applications within it. For instance, an insurance application might have a launch pad with large buttons containing the names of all the insurance policies that can be created, for example: life, health, disability. A launch pad is also a home base of sorts, but on a very high level. In addition to the launch pad, you would also need to pick at least one home base screen for each of the individual applications. For example, life on the launch pad would need its own home base screen.

Identify How Users Access Main Windows

How do users access main objects? Are the main window and its object displayed when the system is powered up? Or are main task objects represented as window icons on a desktop or workspace that must first be opened by the user?

Will the interface be object-action oriented or action-object oriented? For example, does the user open a memo directly, or first open an editor and then load a memo? Object-action oriented interfaces allow users to focus on their task and not be so aware of the operating system and separate applications. Many legacy systems are based on action-object orientation, which is often *not* the most intuitive way to organize your interface. Having users first choose an object to work on (a particular customer or contract), and then having them decide on the action to take (open it, add some data, print it out) often results in a better design.

You will need to decide on how flexible your interface is for different users and tasks. Do not be fooled into thinking that maximum flexibility is always best. If users are under a lot of stress and need to do some tasks quickly and infrequently, then it may be best to lead them through step by step without a lot of flexibility. If, on the other hand, they need to complete simple tasks quickly and in an unpredictable order, you may want to build in a lot of flexibility. Figure 3.8 shows flexibility as a continuum with no particular right or wrong point. You will need to decide for your particular application, task, and user groups.

Assign User Actions for Main Windows

User actions are the commands that will be represented in the interface as drop-down menu options or graphical controls or typed commands. These will be of two types:

1. Actions users will want to perform on the object represented in the window. You will have this information ready as a result of your user object work.
2. Actions that could take advantage of the magic of computers and facilitate the users' task (for example, Undo, Sort).

Look for actions that might be common across windows (objects) and could use the same name (for example, Print, Save). You should have most of the actions of type 1 already documented. But you may have new ones of type 2, or you may have made some modifications to the type 1 actions as you were storyboarding in previous steps.

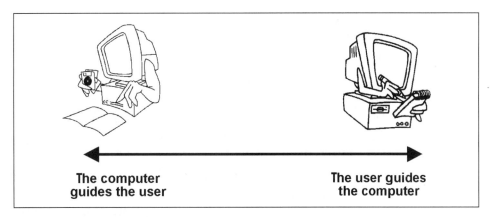

Figure 3.8 Flexibility is a continuum.

In order to make decisions about actions and how they should be made available, make a list of all actions that are in your main windows and home bases. If the action refers to viewing an object that is part of the window design, there are no further actions the user needs to take to accomplish his or her task. Therefore the action does not need to be part of the table. For example, the action of viewing the running balance on the bills worksheet is not on the action table shown in Figure 3.9 because it was designed to be displayed in the window at all times. Figure 3.9 shows some of the actions for the Check-Ease windows.

Action	Command Button	Toolbar	Menu	Other GUI Widget
Run a report				
Open the bills worksheet				
Save the bills worksheet				
Enter a new bill				
Change amount to pay				
Delete a bill				

Figure 3.9 Action table showing actions for the Bills Worksheet in Check-Ease.

Next, make decisions about the actions. Trade off ways to present the different actions to users, such as drop-down menus, pop-up menus, fixed menus, toolbars, or command buttons. Consider the following:

❑ *Frequency of use.* Which actions will users need to perform very frequently? These actions might best be presented to users as graphical buttons and tool palettes that are always visible and available on the screen. Less frequently needed choices can be presented in pull-down and pop-up menus.

❑ *Interface style standard.* Which of the needed actions match the standard menus and menu options found in the style guide? Use the same menus and menu option names when users can benefit from conformance to the standard (that is, they already use or will use other applications that conform to this look and feel). However, do not force-fit needed user actions or user terminology into the standard's structure where the match is not good.

❑ *Amount of direct manipulation.* Decide how much direct manipulation will be supported. For example, will users print a document by using a mouse or trackball to drag a document icon and drop it on a printer icon, or will they select a print option from a drop-down menu, or can they do either?

❑ *Keyboard support.* Heads-down data entry users and touch typists will want to use keyboard equivalents and accelerators for window manipulation actions and frequently used menu options. These allow them to bypass use of the mouse and keep their hands on the keyboard.

Document your decisions by completing an action table. Figure 3.10 shows part of the Action Table for the Bills Worksheet.

After you have identified user actions you can identify interaction techniques. Interaction techniques are how users will use available input devices to perform needed actions. For example, a menu option can be selected by pointing a mouse-controlled screen cursor at the menu option and clicking a mouse button, by typing some combination of keyboard keys, or both. Depending on the user interface design constraints, available input devices will include a keyboard, mouse, trackball, or touch screen.

Action	Command Button	Toolbar	Menu	Other GUI Widget
Run a report		✔	✔	
Open the bills worksheet		✔	✔	
Save the bills worksheet	✔		✔	
Enter a new bill				Select & edit row
Change amount to pay				Select & edit row
Delete a bill			✔	Select & edit row

Figure 3.10 Part of the Actions Table for the Check-Ease application, with columns completed.

Create Design Mockups

When you have made object, metaphor, representation, and action decisions, you are ready to create design mockups. Design mockups take all your decisions to date and document them with a lo-fi paper prototype.

Your goal in creating the design mockups is to document all the decisions, show how they fit in with actual screens, and prepare a paper prototype that can be shown to others. You can use your earlier storyboards to start, but you will need to redo the storyboards in light of your high-level design. This is also the time to go back and build in some of the exceptions (tasks with low frequency) that you passed over during storyboarding. Just as in storyboarding, however, you should involve both users and technical people at this stage.

Figures 3.11 through 3.15 show design mockups of some of the screens for the Check-Ease application.

Use the mockups to show:

❑ How users will perform common work tasks with the new interface

❑ How the interface will portray task objects and offer actions to users

❑ The look and feel of the selected interface style

❑ Alternative conceptual or high-level interface designs

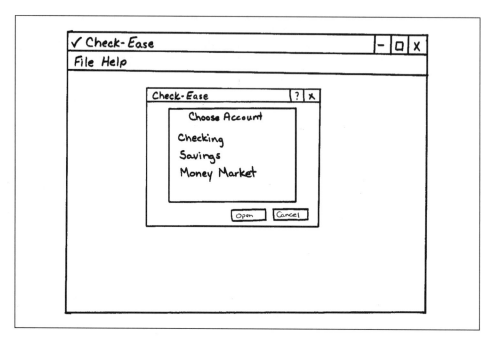

Figure 3.11 Design Mockup of the opening window for Check-Ease.

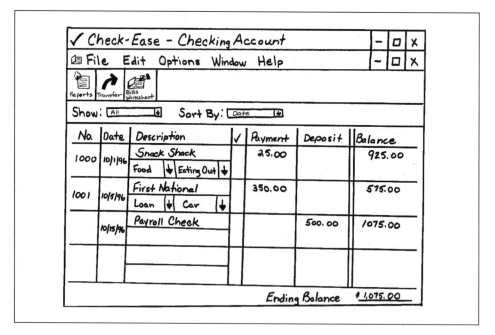

Figure 3.12 Design Mockup of the Checkbook window for Check-Ease.

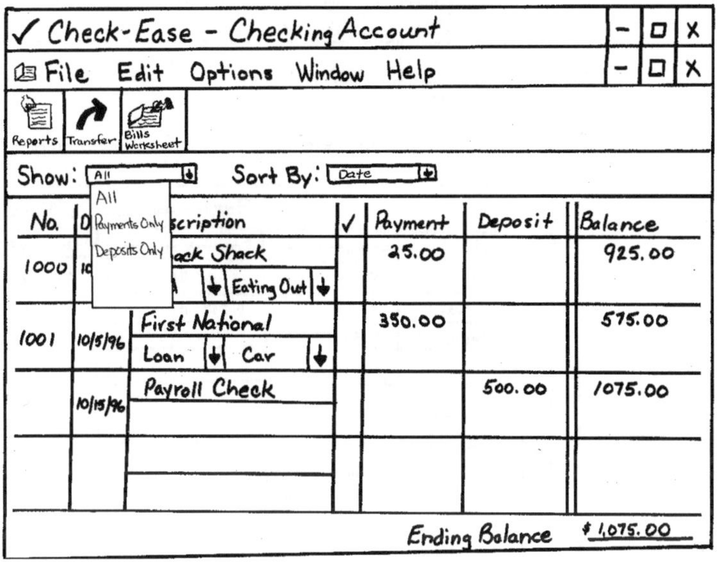

Figure 3.13 Design Mockup showing the Show drop-down list.

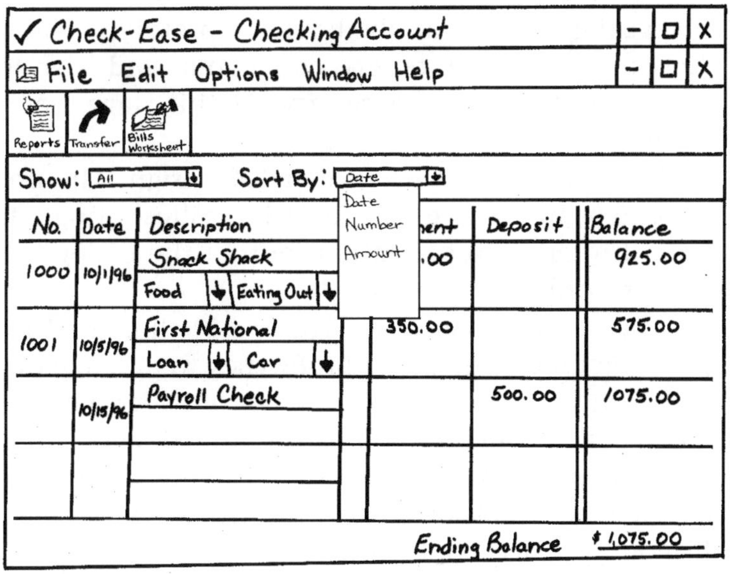

Figure 3.14 Design Mockup showing the Sort By drop-down list.

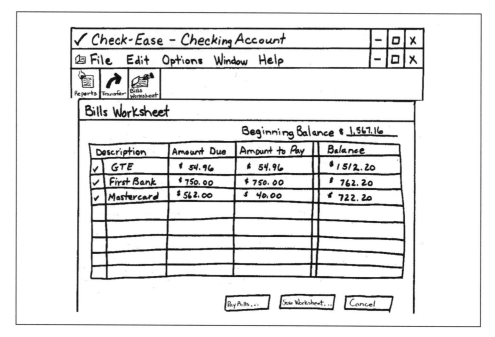

Figure 3.15 Design Mockup showing the Bills Worksheet.

Don't get bogged down in producing a sophisticated prototype. The goal is to very quickly develop a prototype that can be used to review and test the interface conceptual and high-level designs and then change them as necessary. At this stage, you may need to redesign.

Don't get caught up in detailed design. The prototype does not have to be interactive. The focus is on illustrating task objects and the overall interface organization, not all the dialog boxes, detailed layout, or wording.

The mockups shown in Figures 3.11 through 3.15 are copies of paper prototypes. The paper prototypes were made out of construction paper, sticky notes, and other types of paper. There are a lot of different types of materials you can use for design mockups that make it easy for you to show the interface to others. For example, sticky notes allowed us to quickly show what the drop-down menus would look like on the Checkbook Window.

We use paper prototyping kits when we are creating design mockups. These are small cases containing a wide variety of paper, pens, markers, pencils, construction paper, glue sticks, scissors, tape, rulers, and so on. Marc Rettig, in his *Interactions* article "Prototyping for Tiny Fingers," describes paper prototyping and gives a list of items to put in a kit.

You will also be creating the menu bar and toolbars. We use a card technique to help design menus. Each action that is in the menu column of the action table becomes a card. These will be the menu items in the drop-down menus. Use index cards or sticky notes of one color. Cards or notes of a different color are used for menu bar items.

Now you can create the menu system on a table or a wall. If you think you will be using some standard menu bar items, such as File or Help, you can fill those in right away. Other menu bar items you will need to create as you go along. This technique is powerful because it allows you to quickly iterate through many different designs, reorganizing again and again in a short amount of time. It is a good technique to use with a group.

You can design toolbars this way as well. Use a different color card or note for items that you think should go on the toolbar. You can draw quick sketches of the buttons, or just use words. Don't spend a lot of time at this point deciding on a particular pictorial representation.

Review and Revise the High-Level Design

Improve the high-level interface design before trying it out with users. First, test the interface high-level design against your use case scenarios. Evaluate how well the interface organization seems to support how users need to work. Revise the design and associated mockups as needed.

Next, organize a review meeting with the rest of the project team. Using the design mockups, conduct a walk through of key user tasks. Use the walk through to identify:

- ❑ Conceptual design problems, such as task objects that are not easily recognized and confusing task object or action names
- ❑ High-level design problems, such as confusing organization of windows and task flow
- ❑ Interface designer misunderstandings, such as misunderstandings about system scope and interface design constraints

In order to have a productive meeting, you want to encourage participants to give you feedback. If you appear defensive or argumentative you will discourage people from speaking their minds.

Don't use the meeting to revise the interface design. Take notes on participant comments and suggestions, but don't attempt to redesign the interface on the spot. Based on the feedback received in the review meeting, improve the high-level interface design and revise the associated mockups. Hold another design review meeting if needed.

Test

You can get feedback from users in an informal walk-through process using your design mockup. You can also conduct a usability test on a lo-fi paper prototype. See the section in the Usability Testing chapter on how to conduct a usability test on a paper prototype.

We are sometimes asked why we don't go right to hi-fi computer prototyping at this point. Or why didn't we go right to it as soon as we were ready to mock up the design? It is very important that you develop a hi-fi computer prototype, but there is critical information you need to get and react to first. You must test your conceptual design to make sure it is intuitive to users. As soon as designers sit down in front of a computer the dynamics of design change. Research, as well as our own experience, shows:

- ❑ *It takes too much time.* You need to be able to quickly get a lo-fi paper prototype in front of people and get feedback and make changes. Putting a design online takes more time.

- ❑ *It looks too polished.* People actually give less feedback because a computer prototype looks so finished. A lo-fi prototype is done with paper, and is obviously not a complete design. You get more and different types of feedback from users with a lo-fi prototype. At some point you want a polished look. But at this point in design you want feedback on your conceptual design more than the exact layout of screens.

- ❑ *Designers become resistant to change.* Your ideas need to still be fluid at this point, and going on computer with the screens starts to solidify them. As soon as you go online there is a subtle but significant resistance to making changes.

❑ *Loss of focus on the interface.* Going to a computer prototype gets everyone on the team away from the interface and starting to worry and think about implementation, technical issues, and so on. These are important issues to deal with later, but at this point they will take away from interface design.

You want to get as much feedback as possible, as quickly as possible. Preferably, you want to get feedback from users and key stakeholders, make changes, and get feedback on the changes. Make sure that as you get feedback, you are involving representative users that have *not* been involved in design up to this point. You cannot use only the users that were part of the interface design team—they are not typical users anymore.

Make sure you get feedback from any key stakeholders. Although they might not be actual users, if their approval is critical, make sure they see the design at this earlier stage.

Develop the Support Plan

An important principle of user-centered interface design is the principle of integrated design. The user interface is more than just screens or windows and messages, it is all the system elements users come in contact with and that give them ideas about how the system works and how to use it. The user interface, then, includes user documentation and training.

A common mistake when developing a new interface for a system is to assume that easy-to-use screens will mean no user training will be required. Another common mistake is to assume that online help is the best and only type of user support needed. A walk-up-and-use interface designed for ease of learning may indeed require no training (for example, automated teller banking machine). But this style of interface is inappropriate for complex applications and frequent users where ease of use will be more important than ease of learning. Most interfaces will require some kind of user support. User support can take many forms:

❑ Job aids (such as quick reference cards and keyboard templates)
❑ Classroom training

- ❑ Reference manuals
- ❑ On-the-job training
- ❑ Computer-based training (for example, tutorials, cue cards)
- ❑ Hot line
- ❑ Online help
- ❑ Video courses
- ❑ Online manual
- ❑ Workbooks

To document your decisions, develop a support plan. A support plan defines the best mix of online and offline documentation and training for a particular interface and its users, and the information these should contain.

Identify User Knowledge and Skill Deficiencies

Identify and list all the knowledge and skills a user must possess in order to use the system effectively and efficiently. Include both system and task knowledge.

Next, identify which knowledge and skills in the list users can be expected to possess when they first encounter the new system. The knowledge and skills that remain (that users don't possess) constitute deficiencies that must be addressed by support elements. List these deficiencies. Figure 3.16 shows part of the Skills and Knowledge list for Check-Ease.

There are several ways to gather information on deficiencies:

- ❑ Review the user profiles.
- ❑ Have documentation and training specialists walk through the mockups and prototypes.
- ❑ Watch users try to use the mockups and prototypes, and note what they do and don't know how to do.

Map the Support Plan

After you have identified the knowledge and skill deficiencies, map these against online and offline delivery or media alternatives. Be sure to involve training and documentation specialists.

Knowledge/Skill	Users Already Possess?
Start up MS Windows	✔
Mouse/trackball/keyboard Use	✔
Graphical controls use	✔
Install Check-Ease	
Modem hook-up and software installation	
Hypertext help navigation	✔
Connect/Disconnect with bank	
Create a Register	
Make a register entry	
Reconcile checkbook	
Print checks	
Run reports	
Hot key use	✔
(etc.)	

Figure 3.16 Needed knowledge and skills for Check-Ease.

Trade off these three types of support for each deficiency; for example:

❑ Training, such as a Getting Started tutorial is required when the knowledge or skill constitutes a prerequisite to using the system.

❑ Job aids like quick reference cards and online help provide memory joggers when using the system.

❑ Documentation (user guides) can provide system overviews and orientation, and support complex decisions and infrequent actions.

Trade off online and offline support delivery media for each deficiency:

❑ Online support can be updated and distributed automatically, quickly searched, and can reduce the intimidation of large manuals.

❑ Offline support can be studied, taken home, and used when the system is down.

Note that the same kind of information might need to be delivered in more than one way. For example, a description of how to use the mouse buttons to perform different interface interactions might be covered in initial training provided by a getting started tutorial and also in a user guide.

The support plan documents your decisions on how online and offline support elements could be used to address user knowledge and skill deficiencies. The map also provides a preliminary list of the contents of each candidate support element. Figure 3.17 shows part of the preliminary Support Planning Table for Check-Ease. The left column lists the deficiencies. The other columns list the possible types of support. A check in a cell indicates that the particular type of support could meet that deficiency. Note that many deficiencies would be covered in more than one type of support.

Deficiency	*Getting Started Tutorial*	*Online Help*	*User Guide*	*Quick Ref. Card*	*Online cue cards*	*(etc.)*
Install Check-Ease			✔			
Modem Installation			✔			
Connect with bank		✔	✔			
Create a register	✔	✔	✔		✔	
Make a register entry	✔	✔	✔	✔	✔	
Reconcile checkbook	✔	✔	✔		✔	
Print checks	✔	✔	✔			
Run reports		✔	✔			

Figure 3.17 Part of the Support Planning Table for Check-Ease.

Review the initial support plan with project management, marketing, and so on with consideration for project budget and schedule constraints. Select a final set of support elements for actual development.

Summary

The Design phase is at the heart of Intelligent Interface Design. The phase starts with information gathered during Analysis and ends with a design mockup. Figure 3.18 is a Design Checklist to help you through the process.

Design Checklist	
✔	*Step*
	Choose major user objects
	Identify objects from analysis documents
	Identify object attributes
	Identify user actions on task objects
	Select metaphors and representations
	Storyboard the major user objects and metaphors
	Create a high level interface design
	Select/adapt a style
	Identify main windows and related user actions
	Identify home bases and launching pads
	Identify how user access main windows
	Assign user actions for main windows
	Create design mockups
	Review and revise the high level design
	Test
	Develop the support plan
	Identify user knowledge and skill deficiencies
	Map the support plan

Figure 3.18 The Design Checklist.

Chapter 4

Construction

Analysis

Identify Scope
Develop User Profiles
Gather Data
Document Current Tasks
Document Opportunities
Describe Future Tasks
Develop Usability Specs
Develop Scenarios
Test

Design

Choose Objects
Select Metaphors
Storyboard
Create High Level Design
Test
Develop Support Plan

Construction

Develop Prototype
Test Prototype
Document the Design

Contents

Purpose

Deliverables

Preparation

Process

Summary

Once you have tested and revised your high-level design mockups you are ready to create a more detailed and realistic version of the interface. Prototypes are the tools for constructing the interface.

Purpose

Construction has several purposes: (1) create a hi-fi computer prototype, (2) further iterate your design and test with users and key stakeholders, and (3) document your complete, final design for the development team.

Deliverables

At the end of Construction you will have:

- ❏ *A hi-fi computer prototype of your interface.* Most windows, menus, and dialog boxes on computer with navigation.
- ❏ *A user interface design description.* This documents your interface design for the development team.

Preparation

In order to carry out the steps of Construction you will need to have all the products from the previous two steps, Analysis and Design. The team for interface construction can be the same as, or similar to, the team for design. Make sure you have a technical person involved to ensure that the interface you prototype can be implemented with the programming tools that are to be used.

You will also want to have available all the standards and guidelines that you will be following, including your platform guidelines, and any enterprise-wide or project-specific guidelines.

Process

There are three steps in the Construction phase:

1. Develop a hi-fi computer prototype.
2. Test the hi-fi computer prototype and revise it.
3. Document the complete, final interface design.

Develop a Hi-Fi Computer Prototype

The objective of hi-fi computer prototyping is to have a detailed design of almost all windows and dialog boxes that can be used to conduct user testing. Early, rapid prototyping of the interface design provides not only a means to test the design with users, but also:

❑ A means to communicate the design to other project team members and client representatives

❑ A way for nonprogrammers to make design contributions

❑ A tangible means to evaluate and tradeoff alternative design solutions

❑ A dynamic, living specification of the design, subject to less misinterpretation than paper mockups

Creating the Prototype

Start with the revised high-level design mockups from the Design phase. Complete the design of the interface by designing the other windows and dialog boxes that would be displayed in the course of interacting with the main windows, that is, detailed design of menus, option dialog boxes, message windows, help windows, and so on.

Construction is the time to do the following:

❑ Decide on exact location for each control on each screen

❑ Decide on exact wording and names of buttons

❑ Make changes in how much is on each screen

❏ Incorporate all your corporate guidelines and standards

❏ Apply intelligent interface design decisions about visual search, cognitive demands, and so on.

Prototyping allows you to test and revise the actual screen layout. You may find that you have too much or not enough information on a screen when it is actually prototyped as a computer screen. Prototyping allows you to try out different layouts in general, as well as screen by screen.

Figures 4.1 through 4.3 show a hi-fi computer prototype of part of the Check-Ease interface.

During the development of the hi-fi computer prototype, consult Part II of this book on detailed design guidelines, as well as any other books on industry-wide standards and best practices you have available (see the bibliography in this book for more titles). Also be sure you are following your own enterprise-wide guidelines or specific project guidelines.

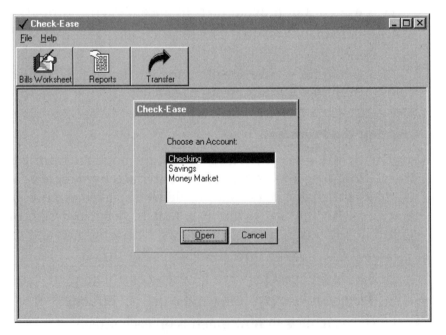

Figure 4.1 Opening screen for Check-Ease.

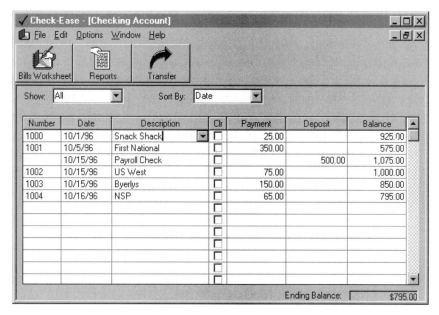

Figure 4.2 Check-Ease with the Checking Account open.

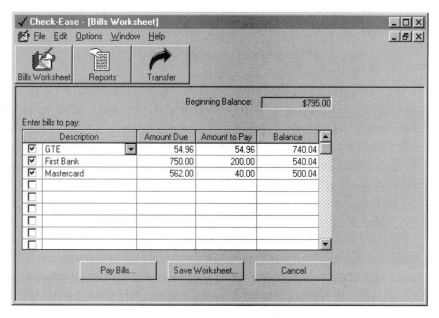

Figure 4.3 The Bills Worksheet.

What Is and Is not a Prototype

It is not critical that the prototype perform data processing, but it should allow users to navigate within the interface (open and close menus and windows) and use graphical controls. The prototype doesn't have to simulate the full functionality of the system.

If you will be using your hi-fi computer prototype in a full usability testing situation, then the prototype will need to be extremely robust, with full navigation and at least simulated data capturing. However, for design reviews, a full working prototype is not necessary.

To avoid common prototyping pitfalls:

❑ *Use an interface prototyping tool*. Choose a tool that facilitates rapid simulation and change of the interface design.

❑ *Don't misrepresent system capabilities and create unrealistic expectations*. For example, you don't want your prototype to suggest unrealistic system response times.

❑ *Don't lose control of the prototype*. The prototype must be a design tool. It is not a marketing or programming tool. You may need to convince others that it doesn't portray the final interface design and must be allowed to evolve and change.

Software is often prototyped for a variety of reasons, including to test out system performance, functionality, or programming tools. But a prototype that is designed to test the interface will be different. For example, if you are testing system performance and response time, you want to simulate entering and retrieving actual data of realistic size from a database to see how long it takes. If you are prototyping to test the interface, however, you do not need an actual database with a full complement of real data.

Be very wary of producing a common system prototype to be used for all purposes. If a prototype for other purposes is planned you might be able to combine it with the prototype you need. But it might take longer to create than you can wait for interface testing. There is also the danger of the project team getting too involved in writing code, and being unwilling to keep making changes through the interface construction phase.

Prioritizing the Prototyping

You may not be able to prototype every screen and dialog box in the interface. Find out what system functions are being developed first. In order to keep up with or stay ahead of the development team, you'll need to prototype and test these first.

You also want to be sure to prototype:

❑ High frequency tasks

❑ The parts of the interface where there is the most uncertainty about usability

❑ Alternative design solutions

❑ Portions of the design that represent design approaches or features used repeatedly throughout the GUI design

Test

Testing during the Construction phase includes design reviews of the hi-fi computer prototype, and usability testing.

Design Reviews

Before you conduct usability testing with users, you need to conduct design reviews within the team and with users and key stakeholders.

First the design team should use the prototype to walk through the user task flows and scenarios developed in Analysis. Evaluate how well the interface design supports how users need to work. Revise the design and prototype as needed.

Next, use one or more of the following techniques to further evaluate the prototype:

❑ A comparison against human factors guidelines and checklists, for example, the guidelines that are in Part II of this book

❑ A review by colleagues not involved in the design of this particular interface

❑ A review by an interface design expert

❑ A review by users and key stakeholders

During these design reviews look for any of the following:

❑ Confusing organization of the interface into windows and dialog boxes

❑ Missing or unclear window, menu, and control labels

❑ Unfriendly, unhelpful wording or messages

❑ Unnecessary steps that slow user interaction and task performance

❑ Confusing, cluttered layout

❑ Misuse of visual coding techniques that hinder visual searching and interpretation (for example, a picture that looks like it is selectable but it is not)

❑ Lack of continuous and clear feedback for all user actions

❑ Noncompliance with the selected interface standards and guidelines

When you are soliciting feedback from participants in design reviews make sure that:

❑ You do not discourage participants from providing valuable feedback by appearing defensive or argumentative.

❑ The meeting isn't used to revise the interface design. Take notes on the comments and suggestions, but don't attempt to redesign the interface on the spot.

Based on the feedback you receive, improve the interface design and revise the hi-fi computer prototype. But where there is doubt or disagreement about a design issue or solution, resolve it through usability testing.

Usability Testing

When you are ready to conduct formal usability testing with your hi-fi computer prototype you will need to make sure it is robust enough to be used to complete real tasks. If you do have a complete and robust prototype, then you can conduct a usability test and collect valuable information on the usability of your interface design with real users in a realistic setting. See Chapter 5, "Usability Testing," for details on how to conduct a usability test.

Based on the results of the usability test, make changes to the prototype and conduct more testing if needed.

Document the Interface Design

After you develop the hi-fi computer prototype, someone is going to have to implement it in code. How do you communicate and document the entire interface design so that the development team knows how the interface should not only look, but also behave?

Prototypes Alone are not Enough

Interface drawings, mockups, and prototypes developed for design and usability testing don't make good design specifications. They are not usually complete, and you have to run the prototype in order to access the specifications. Most importantly, the purpose of interface prototyping is to rapidly turn around alternative design ideas and try them out with users. Spending time developing a fully complete system prototype for documentation purposes will discourage design iteration.

The Problem with Typical Interface Documentation

In the days of character-based interfaces, system design documents often specified a user interface design using a combination of screen drawings or prints and flow charts (state transition diagrams). The problem is that these representations don't work well for describing a GUI. That's because there are typically so many possible screen transitions from a same screen that the resulting diagram is an incomprehensible web.

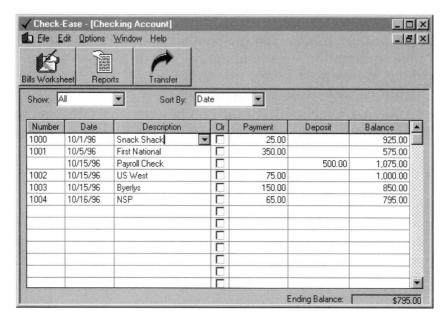

Figure 4.4 Check-Ease screen.

Event	Response
User double clicks window close box	Close window
User selects an item in drop-down list	Change appearance of contents of list box
User selects a different item in drop-down list	Change appearance of contents of list box in a different way
User selects toolbar button	Open new window
User selects list item and an item in a drop-down menu	Some will change appearance of window, others will open new windows

Figure 4.5 Some of the possible transitions for one screen.

For example, refer to figure 4.4. This screen is a window that contains many standard graphical controls, for example, a scrollable list box, drop down list box, command button, and text field.

Just a sample of the possible transitions from this one screen are listed in the table in figure 4.5. This partial list doesn't begin to cover all the transitory changes in screen appearance that accompany user actions, such as the visible changes in controls as their states change (enabled, disabled, selected) or shape changes in on-screen cursors to indicate a time-out or mode.

Some designers have devised special notations and languages for the purpose of describing user interfaces, some with the goal of developing representations that can be converted into code. Unfortunately, these are like programming languages: they have to be learned and are not easily interpreted by the untrained.

The User Interface Design Description

In order to effectively document your interface you need to create a document that:

- Anyone can write—no special language is required
- Anyone can read—for example, marketing people and users
- Completely specifies the appearance and behavior of the user interface and fills in any gaps in the style guides
- Breaks the interface into meaningful pieces that can be used to track development progress
- Fits into the organization's standard world of project documentation, distribution, and control

We have been using a User Interface Design Description (UIDD) as a way to communicate a complete interface design to software developers. A UIDD documents your interface design. It describes the screen objects, and all interactions in detail for each window or screen.

Figures 4.6 and 4.7 show the Overview of the UIDD sample document for Check-Ease.

User Interface Design Description: Check-Ease, Version 1.01

Scope of this Document
This document provides a description of the graphical Check-Ease user interface design for the IBM PC with monochrome or color display. It defines the appearance of Check-Ease user interface screens and how users interact with these screens. It is a *functional* specification and does not address software implementation.

Organization of this Document
This document is divided into six sections:

Section 1: Screen Objects
This section describes the layout of, and user interaction with, the Check-Ease GUI. For the purpose of describing this graphical user interface design, Check-Ease screens are defined in terms of a hierarchy of *screen objects*. That is, graphical objects like buttons and menus, and data make up windows. This hierarchy is only a tool for organizing the description of Check-Ease screens and is not meant to imply any particular software implementation design.

Section 2: Custom Check-Ease Graphical Objects
For the most part, the Check-Ease GUI design uses standard Microsoft Windows graphical objects. However, some custom objects are required to accommodate requirements and constraints specific to the Check-Ease application. The appearance and behavior of these new graphical objects are described in this section.

Section 3: Standard Check-Ease Interaction Techniques
This section specifies how Check-Ease users use the mouse/trackball, mouse/trackball buttons, and keyboard to interact with the Check-Ease screens. Again, the standard Microsoft Windows interaction techniques are used with few exceptions.

Section 4: Standard Command Buttons And Their Actions
This section defines the names and actions of frequently needed command buttons like *Transfer...* that should be used consistently throughout the Check-Ease user interface.

Section 5: Guidelines And Standards For Detailed Layout Of Check-Ease Screen Objects
Most of the detailed design features of the Check-Ease screen objects are already specified by Microsoft Windows (such as shape of buttons, pointer, and so on). This section provides additional guidance to the developer, including standards and guidelines for:

UIDD Overview: Check-Ease - 1

Figure 4.6 Page one of the Overview of the UIDD sample document.

- Aligning graphical objects,

- Standard monochrome and color palette,

- Standard fonts and their use.

Section 6: Standard Terms
This section provides a glossary of standard terms to be used consistently when communicating with users in prompts, labels, messages and documentation.

Conventions and Definitions Used in this Document

Object: Visible element of the screen that displays information to the user and/or the user can select.

Figure: Screen layouts are illustrated in figures attached to this document and referred to by number in the document.

MS Windows Element: Microsoft Windows graphical object that would probably be used to implement a screen object.

Event: A user action or system event that causes a change in a screen object.

Response: How the user interface responds to an event. Combined, events and responses create user-computer dialogs.

Comments: Other design notes.

Bold: Bold text represents the actual text that users would see on the screen (for example, **File** menu name). It does *not* mean, however, that the text should be displayed in bold (text styles are addressed in Section 5).

TBD: A design issue that has not been resolved.

UIDD Overview: Check-Ease - 2

Figure 4.7 Page two of the Overview of the UIDD sample document.

Each section of the UIDD describes a part of the interface in detail. For example, section 1 on Screen Objects describes each object, the object's Windows elements, and the object's events and responses. Figures 4.8 through 4.11 show a part of section 1 of the UIDD for Check-Ease.

Section 1: Screen Objects

1.1 Check-Ease Application Window

The Check-Ease Application Window is the window that is opened when the user starts the Check-Ease application.

Object: Check-Ease Application Window

Consists of:

- Title bar
- Menu bar

Figure(s):

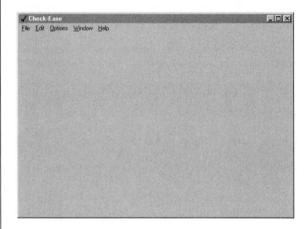

1.2 Checkbook Window

The Checkbook Window is where a user can find and review checks, write checks, balance the checkbook or begin an electronic funds transfer. It presents a register-like view of a checkbook. Users can filter the list of checks to only show, for example, deposits or withdrawals. Checks can also be sorted by date or amount.

Object: Checkbook Window

Consists of:

- Toolbar
- **Show** field
- **Sort by** field
- Register

UIDD: Check-Ease - 1

Figure 4.8 Page one of the UIDD for Check-Ease.

Figure(s):

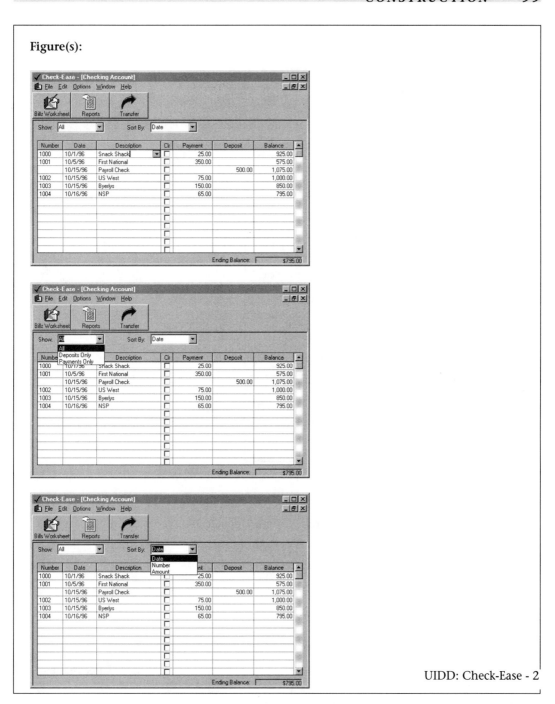

UIDD: Check-Ease - 2

Figure 4.9 Page two of the UIDD for Check-Ease.

MS Windows Elements:

Interface Object	MS Windows Element
Checkbook Window	Primary window with window controls
Toolbar	See Toolbar object
Show field	Drop down list
Sort by field	Drop down list
Register	See Register object

Events:

Event	Response(s)
User opens a new or existing checkbook (see Application Window, *File* menu)	Open Checkbook Window for that checkbook. Title is as was user-defined in **New Checkbook** Window or **Checkbook - Unnamed** If first time opened since application start, **Show** field shows **All**. **Sort by** field shows **Date**.
User selects **Show** field	Open list. Options are **All** , **Payments Only**, **Deposits Only**
User selects **Sort by** field	Open list. Options are **Date**, **Number**, **Amount**
User selects **Close** in **File** menu (Application Window) or User clicks close box	Close Checkbook Window

Object: Register

Consists of:

- **Number, Date, Description, Clr, Payment, Deposit, Balance** column headings
- List box
- **Ending Balance** field

Figure(s):

- .
- .
- .

UIDD: Check-Ease - 3

Figure 4.10 Page three of the UIDD for Check-Ease.

MS Windows Elements:

Interface Object	MS Windows Element
Column headings	Read-only text
List box	Multi-column, single-select list box. See standards for aligning data in columns.
Ending Balance field	Read-only text field

Events:

Event	Response(s)

User opens Checkbook Window	Checks shown and order are as shown in **Show** and **Sort by** fields
	Last entry is blank
	If first time opened since application start:
	    Blank entry is selected;
	    Otherwise, selected entry is same as when window last closed.

User selects **Payments Only** in **Show** field in Checkbook window	Standard drop-down list behavior. Entries in Register that are payments are coded selectable. All others are coded unselectable ("grayed").
User selects **Deposits Only** in **Show** field in Checkbook window	Std. drop down list behavior. Entries in Register that are deposits are coded selectable. All others are coded unselectable ("grayed").
User selects **All** in **Show** field in Checkbook window	Std. drop down list behavior. All entries in Register are coded selectable.
User selects **Date** in **Sort by** field in Checkbook window	Std. drop down list behavior. Entries in Register are ordered from top to bottom oldest to most recent

User selects **Amount** in **Sort by** field in Checkbook window	Std. drop down list behavior.
	Entries in Register are ordered from top to bottom:
	        payments first, deposits second
	        largest to smallest amount

User selects **Number** in **Sort by** field in Checkbook window	Standard drop-down list behavior. Entries in Register are ordered from top to bottom: payments first, deposits second Payments are ordered smallest to largest check number Deposits are ordered by date, oldest to most recent
User selects a Register item and **Delete** (**Edit** menu in Application Window or Delete key on keyboard)	Open **Delete this Entry?** message window (see that object)
(etc.)	

Figure 4.11 Page four of the UIDD for Check-Ease.

As you can see, section 1 of the UIDD is a very detailed description of all the screen objects and their events and responses. To develop this description:

❑ *Document screen objects.* In the section of UIDD regarding screen objects, identify all the major screen objects in the interface. Typically these are the main or primary windows. Then decompose these objects into all their constituent objects and stop when you reach standard GUI objects (widgets). For each object, print or draw all the key views of that object. The more figures the better. Use them to illustrate the object descriptions.

❑ *Document events and responses.* For each object, describe everything that happens as an event and response. In our Check-Ease sample, the UIDD would list every possible event for the Checkbook Window and the resulting changes in the interface. The order in which the events are listed is not critical. Only list the user-perceivable events. Other invisible system events are not described in the UIDD.

Each of the other sections of the UIDD contain a similar level of detail. This ensures that the design team implements the interface the way you intended.

If the system will generate printed reports, the UIDD should include a section on report design descriptions that describes the report layouts.

Wherever possible refer to the style guide or other sections of the UIDD. For example, use the phrase "standard option button behavior" or "standard color palettes" rather than redundantly describing information.

Be sure not to tell software developers how to do their job: The UIDD describes the interface's appearance and behavior, not how to design and implement the software.

About System Implementation

Even though you have thoroughly documented the design, you need to plan for how you will work with system developers as they implement the interface. There will inevitably be questions on the design, as well as possible changes or tradeoffs during coding. You will want someone from the interface design team to be involved and participating during development to keep the interface design perspective going through till the product is complete. This is not really a hand-off of the design. Plan to meet with the development staff regularly, and to review the work as it progresses.

Summary

At this point you will have developed a full interface design: a series of screens that match the way the user is going to work with the new system. The interface portrays objects intuitively and nicely supports user actions. The interface has been tested and revised several times. This is an interface that will be usable, and will not need a lot of changes once it is coded.

Figure 4.12 is a checklist for Construction:

Construction Checklist	
✔	*Step*
	Develop the hi-fi computer prototype
	Conduct design reviews
	Revise prototype
	Conduct usability tests
	Revise prototype
	Create a User Interface Design Description

Figure 4.12 The Construction Checklist.

Usability Testing

Usability testing is not the blessing of the interface.

Contents

Identify the Scope of the Test

Plan and Prepare for the Test

Conduct the Test

Analyze and Report Test Results

Summary

105

Figure 5.1 Usability testing is not the blessing of the interface.

A usability test is a method for finding problems with an interface. The goal of usability testing is to find as many problems as you can during the test, so that you can correct them before a product is released. Usability testing should not be used as a "blessing," or something you do at the end of product development, like a seal of good interface design (Figure 5.1). Usability testing is a tool to help you fix and/or refine a product.

Throughout the chapters on each phase of Intelligent Interface Design, we have discussed testing specific to that phase. In this chapter we cover usability testing methods in general.

Usability testing assumes that some design has been developed and prototyped. Often a usability test is performed on a detailed hi-fi computer prototype. But you can also use a lo-fi paper prototype if you want to test at earlier points during design. There are no exact rules about when to test or how much to test. Some projects require no usability testing at all. Others require or have resources for only one test. Others allow for two or more. Factors to consider when deciding how much and when to test include:

❑ *How new is the design?* If your interface is very different from what users are used to, you may want to test early and often to refine the interface before committing major programming time.

❑ *How accessible are your users?* If your users are not very accessible you may not have a lot of chances during the process to perform usability testing.

❑ *How critical is the interface?* If the interface is for a product that is the main revenue for the enterprise, or for which there is tough competition, then it will be important to do more than one round of testing, and to test as early as possible.

Here are a number of myths about usability testing:

Myth #1: You need an expensive usability lab to do usability testing. You can conduct a usability test with a terminal and two chairs in a relatively quiet place. If you are fighting a political battle, however, there is nothing quite as powerful as an edited, composite 15-minute video showing ten people having the same problem with an interface. A report documenting the test is powerful as well. For these situations you do need a fully equipped lab.

Myth #2: You should test at the end of the development cycle before the product goes out the door. It is still common for usability testing to occur right before the system is released. But what if your test shows there are problems? You should instead test early and test often with both lo-fi paper and hi-fi computer prototypes. That way you can adjust and fix and test again before the software is released. The earlier you find interface problems the easier and less expensive they are to fix.

Myth #3: You should test everything you can. If you just sit users down in front of software and ask them to use it you'll be overwhelmed with data and information to analyze later. Decide on three to five frequent and/or critical tasks to test during a particular session. Then you can get answers on this group of tasks, make changes, and conduct another usability test, if necessary, to check some of these again, as well as other concerns that weren't tested in the first round.

Myth #4: You need to test 100 people. All you need to test is ten people *if,* and this is a big if, they are representative of your real users. Testing ten people who are truly representative will capture 95% of the problems.

Myth #5: A "good" test means no changes are necessary. The only criterion for a successful usability test is whether you get lots of good data on the areas you wanted to test. A blessing from users is not useful to you—you want to find the interface flaws. So be prepared and welcome feedback—even, and especially, negative feedback.

Myth #6: Usability testing is the same as system testing. Usability testing is not the same as system testing. You are not trying to find bugs in the software. You are looking for problems in the interface that affect how easy it is to use and/or learn.

Myth #7: Usability testing is the same as a design review. Design reviews are an important part of the interface design process, but they are not the same as usability testing. During a design review you walk users and/or key stakeholders through the prototype or completed application and get opinions and ideas. This is extremely valuable, but is not the same as giving people realistic tasks and seeing if they can accomplish them, which is what a usability test is all about.

To perform a usability test that will provide you with meaningful and useful data, you should perform the following steps:

1. Identify the scope of the test.
2. Plan and prepare for the test.
3. Conduct the test.
4. Analyze and report the results.

Identify the Scope of the Test

Usability testing means different things to different people. Before you begin a usability testing project, you should discuss the project with key stakeholders and decide upon the scope and purpose of the particular test.

Decide on the Medium

You can perform a test on a completed application, a hi-fi computer prototype, or a lo-fi paper prototype. If you want to test existing software before beginning the design of a new release, your test will probably be conducted using the full version of the software, running on a computer.

If you want to test for interface design problems earlier in the cycle, however, you will need to use a prototype. A hi-fi computer prototype means that the interface is being displayed on a computer, although the entire application is not completely coded. Hi-fi testing can be extremely powerful in testing the interface designs before they are fully implemented. But if you use a hi-fi computer prototype it has to be a working model—during the test people will have to be able to perform actual tasks. This dilemma is why some people choose to use lo-fi paper prototypes for usability testing.

The advantage of testing lo-fi paper prototypes is that you can test early and don't have to worry about the robustness of the prototype (a human is present, making the prototype "work"). The kind of information you get is somewhat different with a paper prototype. You are testing the conceptual design of your interface more than actual screen design. But often this conceptual model feedback is the most important feedback you can get.

Decide on Interaction

Usability tests can vary on the amount of interaction that the tester has with the subject. There are two major camps of usability testing. Some testers say that an informal focus group orientation is best—the participant is allowed to ask questions during the test and have a conversation with the tester. This is called high-interaction testing.

Other testers say that there is a time and place for an interactive discussion, but that time and place is during the interviewing or debriefing *after* the formal test. This camp contends that it is best if users are on their own during testing, and cannot be influenced by tester comments. This is called low-interaction testing. Decide ahead of time whether you are going to allow user and tester interaction during the test, and what kind of interaction is allowed.

Low-Interaction Techniques

Because low-interaction techniques allow little or no interaction between the tester and the participant during the test, it is critical that users think out loud during the test, since the tester will not be able to prompt them for information. Instructions for thinking out loud should be included in the pretest briefing. It is also very helpful to have the participants practice thinking out loud by reading a paragraph about it during the briefing. Some participants are very good at thinking out loud, and others are not. The tester may need to prompt the participant if he or she becomes too quiet during the test ("Be sure to think out loud").

If you use a low-interaction method of testing, your postinterview sessions become critical. You will want to have a two-way dialog after the test, in which you ask questions of the participant ("Why did you open the Customer screen at this point?"); you gather critical data after the test by prompting the participant for more information about some of his/her actions.

Although these methods may seem harsh, some of the best information you get during a test is from watching users wander around an interface and talk out loud. Do not be afraid of using low interaction techniques. You will get great information. They are, however, painful to watch since you have to be willing to watch users struggle, confused and lost.

High-Interaction Techniques

In contrast to low interaction, high interaction tests allow the tester to interact with the participant during the test. The tester may ask for clarification on thoughts or actions during the test, or discuss what the user was expecting to see at a certain point. You will have to decide ahead of time when you will intervene, and how much information you will give when the participant asks a question or asks for help. The danger in a high-interaction technique is that the tester will start to do a demo and that the session will turn into a design review rather than a usability test.

Do not assume that if you have a lot of interaction with the participants you are not conducting a usability test. A high-interaction usability test requires the same task scenarios and thinking aloud protocols as a low-interaction technique.

	Low Interaction	*High Interaction*
Computer Media		
Paper Media		

Figure 5.2 Possible combinations of interaction and media.

Select Type of Test

Since there are two basic types of media for your interface, computer (completed system or hi-fi prototype) and lo-fi paper prototype, and two basic types of interaction, low and high, there are four possible ways for you to conduct your test. Figure 5.2 shows the possible combinations of interaction and media in a table.

Computer Media with Low Interaction

In this type of test setting, the tester conducts a pretest briefing and a posttest interview, but during the test there is no interaction allowed between tester and participant. The tester is in another room watching a monitor or through a one-way mirror. In this type of test, the tester can only intervene in certain situations. It is important to decide ahead of time when the tester will interrupt and what they will say when they do. For example, you may decide that if the participant cannot complete a task within 40 minutes, the tester will interrupt and ask him/her to move on to the next task.

A variation on this technique provides a phone in the room for the participant who can simulate calling a help line. The phone rings in the room where the tester is. If the participant is stuck and calls for help the tester typically gives minimal help—usually asking questions like "What are you trying to do?" or giving a small hint such as "See if there is anything on the menu that would help you."

Although these sessions can be painful to watch or run (it's not fun to see people struggle with your design), they can provide very valuable information. Sometimes the most important information a usability test can yield is from analyzing where people go, and what their thought process is as they wander around. Sometimes the most important information is the tangential information you gain when the participant spends 20 minutes trying to solve a problem. Remember, the goal of the test is to *find problems*, not to have participants complete tasks.

Computer Media with High Interaction

In this environment, you are using a hi-fi computer prototype for the testing, but you are also using a high-interaction mode, in which you interact, discuss, and ask questions as the participant goes through the task scenarios.

Lo-Fi Paper Prototype and High Interaction

Using paper prototypes and high interaction allows you to test anywhere with a minimum of preparation. Changes in the interface are discussed and made on the fly on paper. Instead of videotaping, you may use audiotape, or even just take written notes.

Lo-Fi Paper Prototype and Low Interaction

In this technique the tester is sitting with the participant (because the "system" won't work without the tester present), but again, the amount of interaction is limited to briefing and posttest interviewing only. Otherwise the tester remains mute. The reasons for this are the same as for other low-interaction techniques—to force participants to wander and solve problems on their own.

Decide on the Test Environment

After you choose which type of test you are going to run, you need to make a few more decisions about the testing environment:

- ❑ *Will you be testing in a lab?* Or are you conducting an informal test at a desk? An informal test will be faster and less expensive, but not as impressive as a formal lab test. Think about how you will use the information after the test is done, and who you will need to convince.

❑ *Will you be video-taping the test?* It is not necessary to videotape usability testing sessions, but it is recommended. Advantages of videotaping include:

❑ It gives you clear, incontrovertible evidence to back up your results.

❑ You are free from taking profuse notes and missing critical information.

❑ After the test you can go back and study particular tasks to deduce what actually occurred. This aids in making recommendations for changes to the interface.

❑ You have the makings of an excerpt tape. Humans react in powerful, emotional ways to video. You can make your point faster and with 100 times more power by showing ten people in a row having the same problem rather than just showing statistics or describing the events in words.

Here are some disadvantages of videotaping testing:

❑ Videotaping often inhibits the participants. They may tend not to talk as much or be as honest. Try to set up the equipment in a nonintrusive way.

❑ You have one more thing to worry about. You have a great deal to think about when conducting a test. Making sure the video is working properly only adds to the stress. Make sure you pilot the test so you know everything is working correctly. Assign someone to take care of just the videotaping, including labeling videos, checking equipment, and so on.

❑ There will be a lot of data to analyze. If you run ten users through two hours of testing, you will have 20 hours of video to watch. Good logging during the test with logging software will help, but you need to build in plenty of time for watching the tapes during analysis.

Review and Confirm Usability Specifications

In the Analysis chapter of this book, one of the steps is to develop usability goals and specifications. These set the definition of usability. A usability specification describes a particular task that the user should be able to complete and under what conditions. It also describes the criteria the task should be performed against. For example: "The user should be able to customize a standard report and view it on the screen within five minutes the first two times and three minutes thereafter, with online help available." Customizing the standard report and viewing it is the behavior. The criteria is that they should be able to do it within five minutes the first two times and three minutes thereafter. The condition is that online help is available.

Usability specifications are discussed in detail in the Analysis chapter. What is important here is that you review those specifications as you begin planning a usability test. You want to choose the specifications that are to be included in the test. If analysis was not completed on your project, and you do not have any usability specifications to work from, you will have to create some before continuing.

You will not be able to test all your specifications—usually you have many more tasks you would like to test than time will allow. Pick the most important, frequent, and/or critical behaviors, or the ones you are most concerned about.

Choose Participants

Before you decide whom to test, you should discuss and decide on the critical user groups you have and who you need to get feedback from. Typically you have enough time and money to run between eight and ten subjects. Less than six people and you don't have enough data. More than ten you run out of time. But most projects have heterogeneous users—you may have more than one group of users who will be using the software, and these different groups may have different demographics (experience on the job, experience with computers, age, job title, and so on).

You need to review the user profiles that were created during Analysis for your project, and then decide on the make-up of your testing group so that you gather information during the test that is most useful and critical. For example, you may decide to test two people who have experience with the prior version of the software and two who do not. And/or two people from headquarters and two from the field. By reviewing the demographics or profiles of your users, you can then decide on the demographics of the particular test group.

Now you are ready to sign up your participants. Remember to also schedule alternates.

Plan and Prepare for the Test

Once you have your participants lined up, you still have a lot of work to do before your testing can begin.

Create Test Scenarios

After identifying who the users are and the specifications you would like to test, you are ready to decide on specific test scenarios. These test scenarios describe the actual tasks that participants will go through during the test. Figure 5.3 shows a sample test scenario for a usability test on Check-Ease.

In deciding what scenarios and in what order to have them performed, you will need to consider the following:

Task 3: Pay bills

Your Situation: You have six bills that have to be paid. The bills are in a folder on the table.

Your Job:

1. Enter the bills into Check-Ease.

2. Decide whether you have enough money to pay all of them.

3. If you do have enough money, pay them all.

4. If you do not have enough money, pay less on the credit card bill so that you can pay the rest.

Figure 5.3 Sample test scenario for Check-Ease.

❑ *You want to create as realistic a situation as possible.* You want the participants to simulate being at work doing their job. What combination or order of scenarios will make this work?

❑ *You have to create data to match.* You will have to set up the software with beginning data to support the tasks. Some scenarios may entail too much work to simulate. Think through the implications of your scenarios.

❑ *Pick the most critical/important/frequent tasks from the specifications.* You are not going to be able to test all the specifications. Which are most important to you? Find the one or two you must test and then build the rest of the scenarios around those.

❑ *Consider starting in the middle.* Many people are tempted to test an entire procedure from beginning to end. It may be a better use of time, however, to give the participants some beginning data and have them start in the middle of a task and take it through to the end.

❑ *You only have an hour and a half at the maximum.* You probably have even less than that! Two hours total is usually the most time you can bring participants in for. You must allow time for them to get ready, your briefing and posttest interviews, and so on. Usually about an hour or an hour and 15 minutes is all they will really be on the system. Plan accordingly, and put the most important tasks to test first, since not all participants will get to all tasks.

Develop a Usability Test Plan

It is important that you have buy-in from all key stakeholders before you start testing, so a usability test plan is a good way to document all your decisions. A usability test plan summarizes and documents all your work to date. It should include:

❑ *The goals of your test.* You have made some decisions on the scope of your project. Each specific usability test should have a goal statement. For example: "The goal of this test is to test the Customer Service application beta version 4.0 with both new and experienced users."

❏ *Testing schedule.* At this point you should have a specific schedule for the pilot test, actual testing participants, analysis, and presentation of results. Put this schedule in the test plan.

❏ *Testing method.* You need to describe in general terms the type of testing you are doing so others know what to expect. Is this a formal test in a lab? With video?

❏ *Participant demographics.* Describe your decisions on who is participating and how many people are from each demographic group. Include any details you have on individuals.

❏ *Test procedures.* Explain the step-by-step procedures you will use when participants arrive. Include instructions, the testing scenarios, posttesting interviews, and so on.

Prepare Test Materials

Now that you have a plan in place, it is time to prepare materials for the test. Materials may include:

❏ *The prototype.* To conduct your test, you must have a prototype for the participants to use. This can either be a lo-fi paper prototype or hi-fi computer prototype. You will need to make sure that you have a prototype that will work for the scenarios and the order in which you have them. You may also have to figure out how to get the prototype back to "zero state" quickly, for instance, erasing data that a participant enters as part of the test. You may need to change the scenario slightly after you have tried it on the prototype to make the test go more smoothly.

❏ *Test scenarios.* After you have revisited your scenarios with the prototype, you are ready to prepare materials for the participants to use during the test. They may need cards for each task, or one sheet listing all the tasks. Make sure you give them just enough information to do the task, and not step-by-step instructions. For instance, don't write an instruction for them that says "Choose Open Customer from the File Menu." That gives them too much information. You will only be testing your instructions. Say instead, "You are going to enter some data for a new customer. Bring up a form for entering new data." Remember, you are testing the interface, not the functionality of the software. Given realistic work information, where do they have problems performing the task?

❑ *Thinking aloud instructions.* If you provide instructions for thinking aloud and have the participants read them aloud before the test starts, you will find that they understand better what you mean, and also that they are more willing to talk aloud once the test starts.

❑ *Observer forms.* Many usability tests have a veritable parade of people wanting to observe. Make sure you have space for observers to come and go without disturbing the participants or the testers. Try to schedule your observers so it doesn't get too crowded. Put the observers to work by deciding what information you would like to get from them, and putting it on a form for them to fill out.

❑ *Observer instructions.* Observers will know what to do, how to help, how to stay out of the way, and how to give constructive feedback if you provide them with instructions on how best to observe. Having observers is a wonderful way to get buy-in from key stakeholders. Take advantage of this, but be prepared as well.

❑ *Logging software.* If possible, automate your note-taking by using logging software. Logging software is connected to both a computer for note-taking, as well as the video equipment. By using logging software you can record a specific event on the videotape, and attach a note or observation that you make. Check out what logging software is available to you through the lab, if any, and decide who will do the logging. The log is only as good as the person creating it, so put one of your best observers to the task of recording events and observations.

❑ *Video/audiotaping equipment.* Although it is not necessary to tape a test, a permanent record is very useful, and may be critical if you have to later convince others of the need for interface design changes. Decide and plan for how you will record the test. Typically one or more cameras are used in a lab setting to record the participants' face and the computer screen (or paper prototyping screen). Sometimes a third screen is used for the keyboard/mouse. A common technique is to use a scan converter to record the computer image and mix it with the video from the cameras.

Although video is powerful, it is actually the audio of people talking out loud that has the most information and the most impact. Pay attention to the audio quality of your recording, and make sure you are capturing people thinking aloud.

- ❏ Survey forms. You may want to prepare a survey form to have participants fill out. This allows them to give direct answers to specific questions and to quantify their reactions.

- ❏ Briefing instructions. Prepare beforehand the instructions you are gong to give to each participant. Exactly what will you tell them? It is important that each participant receive the same instructions. Don't rely on your memory; write down what you need to say. Some items to include in your briefing are:

  - ❏ Stress that you are testing the product, not them.
  - ❏ Tell them you are looking for problems in the product.
  - ❏ Let them know if online help is available, or how to use the phone help if available.
  - ❏ Tell the participant it is okay to quit at any time.
  - ❏ Talk about the equipment in the room.
  - ❏ Explain how to think aloud.
  - ❏ Demonstrate thinking aloud and have them practice.
  - ❏ Explain how much help you will provide (or that you will not provide any if you are using a low-interaction technique).
  - ❏ Briefly describe the tasks and introduce the product.
  - ❏ Ask if there are any questions.

- ❏ *Confidentiality and permission forms.* You may need participants to sign a form that the prototype they see is confidential and give them instructions on what can and cannot be discussed with others after the test. You should have them sign a permission form that allows you to use the test results and audio and video tapes of their test.

- ❏ *Posttest interview list.* Prepare a list of questions to ask and points to go over after the participant is done with the scenarios. During the posttest you can:

  - ❏ Ask questions about some of their actions.
  - ❏ Ask direct questions or for opinions.

❑ Clarify some of the comments they made.

❑ Ask a set of prepared questions you have created.

❑ Ask them to fill out a survey form.

❑ Thank them for their participation.

Be sensitive of a participant's feelings after a test. It is sometimes surprising how emotionally they react, especially if they were struggling to complete the tasks. Participants seem to need to know that what they did was valuable, that their questions, comments, and problems were just what you were looking for, and that other participants have responded in similar ways. If they had a hard time with the scenarios they will feel that they are to blame. You need to remind them that you were testing the product, not them.

Run a Pilot Test

It is essential that you run a pilot test. The pilot should be a real test in the same environment you will be using for the rest of the participants. During the pilot test you will check out your equipment, your prototype, your scenarios, and your timing. The pilot should be run with a real user, not just yourself testing. You will only be able to find true problems if a real user who is like the rest of the real participants goes through the materials. It is possible that you may need to make some changes in your prototype or your scenario based on the pilot.

Conduct the Test

After you run the pilot and make any last-minute changes you are ready to run the real participants through. Usability testing is intense. If you can, team with others to take turns running subjects so that you will avoid getting too burned out. Don't try to take extensive notes if you have video or audio—you will do best to just observe and stay on top of the test. If you are doing a more informal test and are taking notes instead of taping, make sure you have at least one person whose job it is just to take notes (not to interview, run equipment, and so on).

When you are conducting the test, you will:

1. Greet the participant.
2. Introduce yourself.
3. Cover the items on your briefing form.
4. Have the participant fill out any necessary pretest forms.
5. Conduct the test.
6. Have the participant fill out any necessary posttest forms.
7. Hold your posttest interview.
8. Thank the participant.

Analyze and Report Test Results

When you are done with the tests you will have reams and reams of data. The best way to analyze the information seems to be individualistic: some people like to start by organizing their observations and thoughts, others by digging into detail. The sheer amount of data can be overwhelming. Here are some tips to help you make it through:

❏ *If you were the one to actually run the tests, give yourself a day or two after the test to* not *analyze results.* You will need a fresh perspective before analysis begins. If you are analyzing the tapes but were not the tester, make sure you watch a few sessions from beginning to end before you start analysis.

❏ *Work on each task one at a time.* Analyzing the problems by each task scenario will be much less intimidating. Read the comments and review recordings for one task. Make notes about major problems for that task. Then go on to the next task.

❏ *Focus first on problems, last on solutions.* Although you want to be able to make interface design recommendations from the results of the testing, it is easier and quicker to first identify the problems. For example, make note that most participants could not figure out how to add in a new vendor. But don't worry yet about what the solution is for the problem.

❏ *Keep in mind the goal—you are trying to improve the interface.* This is not the place for comprehensive research. Rather than get overwhelmed with analyzing everything, stay focused on what is important. You do not have to provide detailed and exacting statistics (53% of participants, and so on). Broad brushstrokes are much more useful (for example, about half of the participants, most people, no one, and so on).

Develop a Preliminary Report

Work first on a preliminary report, rather than trying to develop a detailed comprehensive report right away. This will help you stay focused, move more quickly through critical problems, and get some information right away to all the people that are questioning you about what happened.

Figure 5.4 shows the beginning of a preliminary report. The report lists major problem areas that your test uncovered. It does not organize the problems into categories or make recommendations for change. These steps are done when you prepare the final report.

Findings

Based on the usability test, our preliminary findings are that the product has a small number of problems that critically affect usability, and a moderate number of problems that are not critical, but should be addressed. In general, the participants were favorable towards Check-Ease.

Below is a summary of findings. More detail will be provided in the Final Report.

Difficulty remembering how to switch to a different account.
Participants did not always remember how to switch accounts. Some thought they had to exit all the way out of Check-Ease and come back in, because they remembered the opening dialog box.

Didn't know how to delete a bill.
Some participants did not know to press the Delete key to delete a bill from the worksheet.

Figure 5.4 A preliminary report for the usability test on the Check-Ease application.

ID	Log Event	Comment
2	4	Opened wrong window
2	5	Did not see date field
2	6	Pressed wrong button
2	7	Did not know how to change bill amount
2	8	Confusion over delete
etc.		

Figure 5.5 Bad example of a usability test Results Summary.

Develop a Final Report

After writing your preliminary report, you are ready to prepare a final report. Go through your preliminary report and gather your evidence for each problem you are reporting. This might include your broad brush numbers (all participants had difficulty . . .) as well as notes about places on the videotape that are good examples of the problem.

A final report should not just be a copy of the testing log, as shown in Figure 5.5.

You need to group, explain, and prioritize the findings. Most of the time the test scenarios are a good way to organize the report—discussing problems with each task. Usually, however, there are a number of general problems that go beyond or across the scenarios, so you often need a section on general or overall problems. Figure 5.6. shows a sample table of contents for a final report.

For each problem area provide a recommendation for how to fix the problem. You may also want to include consequences of the problem—what will happen if this problem does not get fixed. This helps others interpret the severity of the problem. Figure 5.7 shows an excerpt from the Final Report on the usability testing performed on Check-Ease.

Also include a summary of findings so that readers can quickly scan the list of all your findings. Figure 5.8 shows part of the Findings Summary Table for the Check-Ease usability testing.

Table of Contents

Introduction to the Test and the Report
Summary of Testing Methods
Summary of Participants
Findings and Recommendations
    Task 1
    Task 2
    Task 3
    Task x
General Findings
Summary Table of Findings
Summary Table of Recommendations
Survey Results

Figure 5.6 A table of contents for a final report.

Task 3: Enter bills

Difficulty remembering how to switch to a different account.
Participants did not always remember how to switch accounts. Most
participants thought they had to exit all the way out of Check-Ease
and come back in, because they remembered the opening dialog box.
About half realized later in the test that they could open a different
account without closing Check-Ease.

Consequences
Some steps take longer than they should. First impression is that there
are more steps than there really are.

Recommendations
(etc.)

Task 4: Modify bills

Didn't know how to delete a bill.
About half of the participants pressed the Delete key to delete a bill. Of
the other half, most were looking for a Delete button on the window.

Figure 5.7 Excerpt from the Final Report for Check-Ease usability testing.

Task	Finding
3	Difficulty remembering how to switch to a different account
3	Not sure what saving the worksheet will exactly do
4	Didn't know how to delete a bill
(etc.)	

Figure 5.8 Part of the Findings Summary Table for Check-Ease usability testing.

In order to make it easier for others to discuss and take action on the results, it is useful for you to prioritize the problems and recommendations in a recommendations summary table. Consider a Critical, Important, and Should Be Changed type of rating. Figure 5.9 shows part of the Recommendations Summary Table from the final report for Check-Ease usability testing.

The goals of creating a final report are to summarize what happened and to provide advice and information that others can take action on immediately.

Creating a Video Excerpt Tape

One of the most powerful actions you can take is to create a video excerpt tape. But be forewarned—these take a lot of time. It is easiest to create the tape after your report, and to have it follow the report. Go by problem area and look for video/audio clips that make your point. This can often be frustrating, because you need short "sound bytes."

Recommendation	Priority
Change wording of Save Worksheet button on the Bills Worksheet	Important
Add Delete button to the Bills Worksheet	Critical
(etc.)	

Figure 5.9 A sample recommendations summary table for Check-Ease usability testing.

Some of the best evidence you have for a problem isn't the best footage for the video excerpt—the sound might not be clear enough, or it takes the participant ten minutes to go through the item you are trying to show.

Make a tape of possible clips for each of the problem areas, then go through and edit, edit, edit. Your goal is to encapsulate 20 hours of video into seven minutes! If you get it down to 20 you have done a wonderful job. Even less is better. Organize the clips for a given problem so that they come one right after another.

If you can, use professional video editing to fade titles in and out for each task and/or problem area. Watch out for quality—second and third generation tapes degrade quickly.

Usability Testing Checklist	
✔	*Step*
	Identify the scope
	Decide on the type of media
	Decide on interaction
	Decide on the test environment
	Review and confirm usability specifications
	Choose participants
	Plan and conduct the test
	Create test scenarios
	Develop a usability test plan
	Create materials
	Run a pilot test
	Conduct the test
	Analyze and report test results
	Develop a preliminary report
	Develop a final report
	Prepare a presentation

Figure 5.10 Usability Testing Checklist.

Preparing a Presentation

Prepare a presentation of your results. You can pass out the final report, show the video excerpt, and go through overheads or a slide presentation of main problems and recommendations. This can be a very political situation, so let the key stakeholders see the report ahead of time so there are no surprises. Since your job is to find problems, your results may not be fully welcomed. Think ahead about how you want to set up the meeting so as to defuse problems and get your message through.

Summary

With planning, a usability test will provide valuable information for what changes your interface needs. Figure 5.10 is a checklist for usability testing.

6

Chapter

Designing for the Web

Contents

Intelligent Interface Design for the Web is in many ways the same as designing GUI interfaces. There are some areas, however, which are different. This chapter describes each of the phases of design for Web sites.

Designing for the Web is relatively new, compared to GUI design. Whenever a new technology emerges there is initially a blending of analysis, design, and development. When GUIs were first under development, most organizations did not separate interface design from software design. Designing a GUI meant creating screens and coding them instantly. Over the last five years interface design has been increasing in sophistication—so much so that there are now phases of interface design.

Internet and intranet applications are now the relatively new technology, which means they are in the blended stage. Designing a Web site to many people still means designing, creating content for, and programming the site. As Web work becomes more sophisticated, however, the need to separate design, specifically interface design, from other components, such as programming, will emerge.

Designing a Web site is designing an interface. The constraints and opportunities are different. The purposes of the visitors and their tasks are sometimes different, but it is still designing an interface.

The purpose of many Web sites is different than the purpose of most GUI software. When people use GUI software they are looking for a tool that allows them to get their work accomplished more efficiently. Although some people visit a Web site to get their work accomplished more efficiently, most people have different purposes at Web sites, such as looking up a particular piece of information, browsing or window shopping, or being entertained. This means that the process of design is different too.

To design an effective, entertaining, interesting, and useful Internet or intranet site requires a blend of skills: graphic design, information design, computer interface design, and Internet programming skills. In addition you will need content experts/sources, and, of course, visitors (users) to give you feedback and to be part of design. This means you must use a team of people, each of whom adds a needed piece.

Chapter 11 in Part II on Internet and intranet guidelines describes design aspects of the sites themselves. This chapter covers the process of effective Web design.

Analysis for Web Sites

Analysis for Web sites is somewhat different than the Analysis phase described in this book for GUI interfaces. Each step is described below.

Identify Current State and Scope

Web sites do not usually have as much history behind them as do GUI projects. This is both a plus and a minus. On the one hand it means less time spent trying to decide on work in progress, what analysis has been already done, and so on. On the other hand it also means that the purpose or reason for the site may not be clear and/or agreed upon by all key stakeholders. Determine whether there is clear agreement on the scope of the project before you decide on the scope of the analysis. You may need to do some extra analysis work researching what visitor tasks are supposed to be part of the interface, and who the visitors really are.

You will also need to define your interface design constraints as you do in GUI design. Below are some possible constraints to pay attention to:

❑ *What platforms will they be using*? The majority of the general Web audience is using a Windows platform with Macintosh coming in next. Many people in corporations use a UNIX platform.

❑ *What browsers will they be using*? Will any of your target audience still be using character-based browsers?

❑ *How many will be using Java-capable browsers*? MS Internet Explorer and Netscape Navigator do not respond the same way to all the codes.

❑ *Which browser will you optimize for*? What release levels of browsers will you optimize for? Define the browser level you want to develop for and understand how any browser-specific tags will be treated by other browsers your audience may use. Keep track of changes in browser technology.

❑ *What bandwidth will your visitors be using*? Are your visitors on an intranet with a wide bandwidth or do you need to plan for those using 14.4 modems? (Predictions are that by 1998 most people will have at least 28.8 modems.) You must consider that net traffic and technical problems will affect how fast your pages load. To alleviate these limitations, keep your files small—under 50 KB when possible.

❑ *How will they have their monitors set*? Research shows that most people use their system as it comes out of the box. That means many are using 640 x 480 x 256 color displays, although most systems sold now come standard with 800 x 600 x 256 settings. Some visitors may be limited to a display of 16 colors, especially if they are accessing via an internal LAN at their company. Others may come in with their monitors set at a resolution of 1280 x 1024. You must design your pages so they provide a quality experience regardless of the visitor's display resolution.

Develop User Profiles

There is a tendency in Web site analysis to say that the visitors are "anyone who signs onto the Web." Although the demographics of every possible person who might sign on is indeed broad, you cannot design a Web site for everyone in the world. You will need to get specific and develop profiles for your planned Web visitors.

❑ *Know your audience*. Everything you do on your Web site must be geared to your target audience. Every graphic, every piece of content, every navigation device must meet the needs of the readers of a given page.

❑ *Who are they*? Who do you want to visit your site? Who do you think will find it on their own? Is your target audience young, old, male, female? Educated or not? How much money do they spend? Are they a captive audience from your corporation's intranet, or anyone in the world who might find your site from a search engine? Identify the characteristics of both the audience who you want and the audience that may find you.

❑ *You may have more than one target audience.* You must identify all your potential audiences. You may want to categorize them as primary and secondary. For example: your target audience is teenagers seeking information on colleges and careers. Secondary audiences are their parents and their teachers.

Gather Data

Comprehensive data gathering and task analysis for Web design are the exception, not the rule. There are several reasons for this trend; for example, there is intense pressure to get a site up fast. Also, many of the tasks that people perform using the Web site are not critical to their day-to-day jobs. As in any other interface design, however, the more data you collect, and the better you understand the tasks people do now that are relevant to your new design, the better your design will fit real users and the fewer iterations you will have to do after the site is developed.

One of the most important areas you need to document during analysis is the purpose of the site. In analysis for GUIs the product definition is usually completed before the interface design team begins analysis. But we have found that in many Web projects design starts without documenting or agreeing on the purpose and priorities of the site. Before you begin designing your site, you should:

❑ *Determine the business purpose of the Web site.* Meet with all the decision-makers. Brainstorm and discuss everyone's goals and business objectives. Discuss how the site's worth will be measured. In other words, what is its ROI (return on investment)? What business problem will this site help resolve? Describe the goals, objectives, and business purposes. Make sure there is agreement and buy-in from key stakeholders before you start design. People often have different purposes in mind when they say, "Let's put up a Web site," as shown in Figure 6.1.

❑ *Determine the site's purpose from your audience's point of view.* What do you want your visitors to get from your site? Is that the same as the business purpose? Make sure the two purposes match. Otherwise your visitors will be frustrated when they come, and you will not understand why they do not come back.

Figure 6.1 Designers with different purposes in mind.

- ❑ *Decide what* you *want visitors to get out of their visit.* Do you want visitors to buy products? To get an impression of your corporate image? To apply for an open position? Donate money? Download software? Get technical questions answered? Receive training?

- ❑ *Find out when in their job tasks the visitors will come.* Will they come for the answer to a specific problem they are having while they are working on another task? Or will they come because they are taking a break and looking for entertainment? Are they doing research before writing a report? Are they looking for specific information that will allow them to take action—like finding out what a movie is about before deciding to see it.

- ❑ *Find out where they will be coming from.* Will they find your pages via a search engine or a table of contents? Will they be coming from your intranet? Will they be coming from somewhere on the Internet? If so, they might find you from a search engine, from a link off someone else's site, or because they bookmarked your URL.

Testing

Because Web design does happen quickly and without as much analysis as it needs, it is even more critical that you test and verify your assumptions after Analysis, before you start Design.

Design for Web Sites

Because a Web site is a computer interface, all the steps and guidelines for designing an effective interface for GUIs hold for Web sites. But many Web sites are discretionary—people do not have to use them. This means that a high premium is given to design considerations that bring people in and bring them back. What makes an effective and professional site? What will bring people back? A site that is:

❏ Easy to use

❏ Fast

❏ Fun

❏ Informative, useful, and current

❏ Interactive—visitors control their paths and can communicate directly with you

Detailed design guidelines for the Web are included in Part II of this book. Here are some ideas to consider as you design the interface of your site:

1. *Review the content.* The content you decide on has a big impact on design. Are visitors accessing course schedules? News bulletins?

2. *Visit other sites.* Visit other sites on the Web. Have everyone on the team do the same. Compile a list of your favorites and least favorites. Include sites whose purpose you think is similar to yours. Include some whose purpose is very different from yours. What do you find useful/entertaining/informative about the sites? Identify the design elements that the team shares on their "good" lists and the elements that the team shares on their "poor" lists.

3. *Decide on objects, metaphors, and representations.* You will need to decide on user objects, metaphors, and representations for each of the main content areas you will be including. You need to decide, for example, whether your site is going to be like a book, a magazine, an online catalog. One of the paradoxes of Internet sites is that they are the newest kind of interfaces, but many ignore the basics of effective interface design. This is very evident in the lack of, or very poor, objects, metaphors, and representations they use.

4. *Decide on a look and feel.* Before you design a look and feel take each of the following into account:

   ❑ Decisions on objects and metaphors
   ❑ Type of content
   ❑ Visitor profiles
   ❑ List of favorite and least favorite Web sites
   ❑ Organization color scheme, logos, and so on

   Keeping all of these areas in mind, have your graphic designer create an appropriate look and feel with the team. Have the designer sketch several ideas about what each of the content areas looks like. Realize that you may have a different look and feel for each of the main content areas, although they should all tie together graphically. You may also have to take into account design and content constraints. You may be using an existing paper course schedule, for example, that already has a certain look and feel, and you may need to stay with that as a constraint. Remember that graphic design for paper is very different than graphic design online, and even more different than graphic design on the Web. The Web presents some very difficult graphic constraints due to both tools and the need to run on all types of equipment. Make sure your graphic designers are experienced with Web graphic design.

5. *Storyboard flow and navigation.* Create a map of the flow and navigation of your site. This is where your information designer's expertise gets used. You will need to make decisions about how much to show at one time, what types of hypertext links are needed, and so on. Use your scenarios of how you expect people to use your site.

There is more standardization in the design of GUI interfaces than Web interfaces. On one hand, this means that there is more room for new, different, creative designs that best meet content and visitors' needs. On the other hand, this means that you must make more decisions about the look and feel of the interface. Should you make your links look like buttons? Like command buttons? Should they be unique graphical buttons? Should they just be hypertext words? The increase in possibilities means making more decisions.

Test

Because there are so many possibilities in Web design, it is imperative that you verify and test your designs with people who would really visit your site.

Construction of Web Sites

The current state of construction of Web site *interfaces* is that it is blended and confused with construction of the actual site. Remember that our focus here is on constructing the *interface* for the site, and not the construction of the site itself. During construction you develop and test a hi-fi computer prototype of the interface for your site. Look to the guidelines in Part II of this book for help.

Testing of Web Sites

It is extremely valuable to test Web sites and it is being done more and more. Besides giving test participants very specific tasks to accomplish, as described in Chapter 5 on usability testing in this book, consider testing your design by giving visitors a list of things they could do at your site and observing which they choose and where they go from there.

PART II

Design Guidelines

7

Chapter

Designing for People

Contents

A technology solution is really made up of two systems: the technology system (for example the computer and software) and the human system (the people who use it). When you apply software engineering to designing software you are designing for the technology system. But when do you design for the human half? Making sure your technology solutions take both technology and the human element into account creates a superior system overall.

Humans have strengths and weaknesses. In designing an interface you want to play up the human's strengths, and design to accommodate or minimize human limits. One way that human factors specialists design for people is to take visual, cognitive, and physical considerations into account (Figure 7.1).

The guidelines in this part of the book stem from knowledge accumulated in the last 50 years about people. Specifically, we draw upon our more than 16 years of direct work in the field. Here is an overview

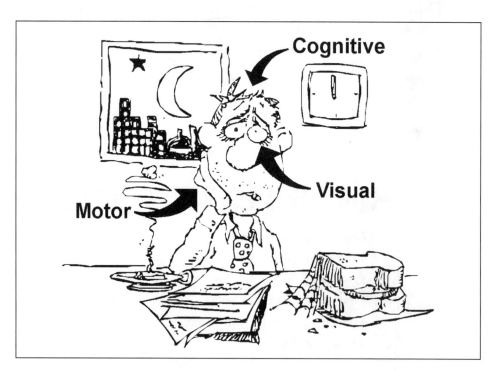

Figure 7.1 Humans have cognitive, visual, and motor limits.

of the guiding principles that form the basis for the interface design guidelines.

Cognitive Considerations

Some of the most important considerations when designing interfaces are the ones involving how people think and learn (cognition). Below are some guiding principles for cognitive processing.

Limit memory loads

People can remember approximately seven new things for about 20 seconds. This is called short-term memory. After 20 seconds they will have lost the information if they cannot quickly store it in long-term memory. Do not require people to remember information longer than this. For example, instead of making a user remember the name of the current customer, show them the name as the user moves from window to window.

One of the powerful aspects of GUIs is that they contain built-in memory aids, for instance, allowing people to choose from a list in a list box rather that typing in data from memory in a data entry box. Make sure you make full use of these opportunities when designing a GUI interface.

Break down decision-making

If users have to make decisions in order to navigate through a task in your software, break down the decision steps into manageable chunks. Have them choose how to sort, for example, and then choose the kind of filtering through a series of controls in a dialog box so that they can think of each decision separately. Use group boxes and labels to help distinguish which decision they should be making at a given point in time.

One of the reasons wizards can be so powerful is that they break down the decision-making to very small steps. This is also one of the reasons they can be annoying—if users don't want such small steps. Be conscious of how small a step your user group needs, and design appropriately.

Provide context

In order for people to be able to understand and remember what is being communicated to them, they need context. Context provides specific meaning and interpretation. If you present information out of context, the material will take longer to be understood and may not be remembered.

Some ways of providing context in a user interface are:

❑ Using titles on screens and windows
❑ Using labels on screen titles, buttons, menus, and group frames that are easily understood (not cryptic abbreviations)
❑ Using menus to show what is available

Be aware of user's mental model

As soon as users begin working with a system, go through training, read documentation, or talk to other people about the system, they begin to create a mental picture or model of how the system works (Figure 7.2). This is a rapid, and not entirely conscious, process. They then use this mental model to predict how the system will behave and to decide what they should do next.

If a mental model is difficult to create, because the interface is so confusing and unpredictable, or the conceptual model it uses is a poor match to how users think about their work, then users will find it hard to learn the system, will make more errors, and will be less satisfied with the system.

To help users learn and use the system, you need to design with the mental model in mind. Part I of this book, especially the section on Interface Design, is concerned mostly with creating a match between the mental model of the user and the conceptual model of the interface.

Figure 7.2 Users create mental models.

Be consistent

One of the ways to facilitate a good mental model quickly is through consistency. People rely on consistency in order to find information quickly, create an accurate mental model, and make decisions. The push to consistency is one reason that platform- and enterprise-specific guidelines are becoming common and important.

Be forgiving

People like to explore and try things out. They will be pushing buttons on the mouse, opening windows, and pressing keys. Make sure your interface allows them to explore without doing damage. Build in ways for users to cancel out, go back, and undo actions.

Visual Considerations

There has been a lot of research on how people scan, read, and find information on screens. If you can reduce the amount of work it takes to visually use a screen, you can save users time and ensure that they'll see critical data. Some overall principles we use in developing guidelines in this area are described below.

Minimize eye movement

Design your screens and windows so that users can start at the top and work their way down without having to move their eyes back and forth or up and down a lot.

Adhere to principles of good format and layout

Research in the field of human factors and screen design has resulted in sound advice on information placement, grouping, and order. Information should be placed to follow the pattern of reading, for example, people who read English will tend to look at the top left of each screen, and then move both left to right and top to bottom. The placement of information on the screen leads them towards either the left to right (horizontal) or top to bottom (vertical) first. Hence, you will see guidelines in the chapters below that say that either a horizontal or a vertical flow is acceptable, but to make sure it is clear which one you are using.

Use color and highlighting judiciously

Don't abuse or overuse color and highlighting. Techniques such as underlining, using boxes, or color can be very powerful ways to visually grab attention. But because they are so powerful, you must be sure you are using these techniques effectively and not overusing them. Every time you use color or highlighting you should be able to state the reason for the particular use. If you cannot find a reason then maybe you shouldn't be using that technique.

Use visual coding

Use visual coding, such as graying out unavailable options to provide visual meaning to data on specific areas on a screen.

Don't assume people will read everything on a screen

If people see things over and over again they *don't* see them anymore—this is called "gating" information. This is a useful function of our brains so that we will notice what is different. But it presents possible problems for the interface designer. You can't assume that people will see or read something just because you put it somewhere on the screen.

Physical Considerations

Sometimes we forget that we require users to interact physically when we design software, for example, manipulating the keyboard, a mouse, touch screen, and so on. Below are some of the critical physical demands to watch out for.

Limit key combinations

Limit the number of combination key presses you require, for example, "CTRL + V." Not only are they hard to remember, they are harder to physically act on.

Avoid difficult combinations

Avoid key combinations that are particularly difficult, for example, requiring users to press three keys simultaneously, or two-key combinations that use only one hand.

Pay attention to touch-typing skills

If users are touch typists they will prefer to keep their hands on the home row. Don't require them to take their hands off this row. If your users are not touch typists, then try to use numbers or function keys rather than letters on the keyboard. People who are not touch typists may have a hard time locating a specific letter.

Avoid a 50/50 split

Avoid forcing users to use a keyboard 50% of the time and a mouse, pointing device, or touch screen 50% of the time, with frequent switching. Although you can use options and choices, you should design for 80% use one way or the other for a particular task.

Watch out for repetitive motion syndrome

Wrist and finger problems resulting from improper use of a keyboard or a mouse are real and significant. If users will be typing or using a pointing device for long periods (greater than one hour), make sure someone will take care of proper support, such as wrist rests, and rest breaks.

Make sure users get training on devices

Don't assume everyone knows how to use a trackball or mouse. Make sure someone is handling training, especially if the device is not standard, such as the pointing device for notebook computers.

Environmental and Social Issues

Don Norman from Apple talks and writes extensively on the ways that computers and technology fit in or don't fit in the social aspects of people's lives. These social considerations are probably some of the most powerful ones in software design, and the most overlooked. In his book *Turn Signals are the Facial Expressions of Automobiles*, Norman comments that people have come to expect that computers will follow the same rules of communication that exist for human to human interaction. In other words, people expect a relationship with computers and with their software. They expect your interface to communicate with them, be flexible in working with them, give them feedback, and so forth. These expectations only increase as interfaces improve.

Many years ago, people were impressed and satisfied if a computer could crunch numbers and produce the correct answer. Now people expect their computers to respond to them conversationally, to be predictable and reliable, and to be friendly and intelligent. This places an even greater amount of work and careful design onto the shoulders of the people who design and create software.

In addition, we need to consider the social, psychological, and physical environment that people are in when they are using our software. Following are some ideas to think about.

Gauge emotions

People react to everything with emotion (Figure 7.3). They decide that they "like" or "trust" your interface, even if they can't tell you exactly what that means. You need to take these emotions into account when you design. Users may have had a negative or positive experience with a previous system and tend to generalize those emotions to your new system. Knowing about likely emotional responses ahead of time will help you plan for them and deal with them up front.

Build in predictability

Although people may want part of their lives to be spontaneous, they want their computers to be very predictable. If they are trying to get work done they will want to be able to predict how the computer will respond to each of their actions.

Figure 7.3 People get emotional about their system.

Watch out for stressful environments

People react to all stimuli differently if they are under stress (Figure 7.4). A screen that may be fairly easy to use can become difficult if the person has someone on the phone yelling at them. Analyze the amount of stress that will be in the environment when people are using your interface. Then analyze the amount of information and the type of activities your interface requires. If users are under stress you may need to make design decisions (such as amount of information on the screen or amount of navigation back and forth) to compensate for the confusing effect the stress will add.

In 1989 an American Navy ship accidentally shot down a commercial Iranian jet. The Navy people on the ship mistakenly identified the jet as a military plane. Shortly after this incident the then head of the Navy said on the radio that all the information the Navy crew needed to make a correct decision was on the computer terminal screen on the

Figure 7.4 Stress affects how people react to stimuli.

ship. But in the stress of the situation they could not find the critical information. "We need human factors engineering on our computer screens," he said. This is an example of how a stressful environment can affect use of a screen.

Consider social interaction

If people are using your software while they are also interacting with another person, you have to be aware of the impact your interface has on the social interaction of the situation. For example, a salesperson speaking with a customer does not want to be distracted or have the customer be distracted by the computer. If the interface becomes a distraction to the interaction between the humans, then it has meddled in the social interaction in a negative way (Figure 7.5). Think carefully how introducing a computer into an existing social interaction may affect the interaction as a whole.

Give some thought as to how people are interacting with others as well; for example, is your user on the phone with a customer while us-

Figure 7.5 Computers should not be a distraction in social situations.

ing the software you are designing? If so, the customer will expect a fast response time from the user. The user may get flustered if it takes a long time to navigate through screens to provide an answer. This in itself can set up a stressful situation, especially if the customer is impatient or upset.

The Purpose of the Interface

For many years users have viewed software as a tool to get their work done. And for many years designers have tried to design good tools. Thinking of software as a tool is still important in many of today's interfaces. Most of Part II of this book deals with guidelines for designing a good tool.

Over the last several years, however, there has been an increase in the variety of purposes people have in using computers. Users now not only want to get their work done, but also want to search, browse, buy, learn, and be entertained. Below are some design guidelines to follow when trying to match the user's purpose.

As a tool

If your users are using your software as a tool to get a much larger job done, they want a useful, reliable, and nondistracting tool. As the designer, you'll tend to see the interface and the software as an integrated, important world. You need to shift your mindset so you can view your interface as a tool, and ask whether it is being useful as a tool. When designing a tool interface, remember to:

- ❑ *Reduce the demands on the user*. Design the screens, windows, flow, and navigation to minimize the number of decisions, amount of searching, amount of thinking and remembering the user has to do. When the purpose of an interface is a tool to get work done, simple is better, boring is good.
- ❑ *Match the user's work flow*. Make sure you know how the user is going to do the work when the new software is in place, and design for that work flow. Don't make them change optimal flow just to fit your order of screens.
- ❑ *Follow standards*. Minimize the learning time by incorporating industry-wide and enterprise standards for screens, menus, and controls.

Searching

Sometimes the user's main purpose at a given moment is to search for information. This might be searching for a particular file or report, searching for data, or searching for information through online catalogs. When users are searching they need to be able to change their minds frequently, go back and forth between detail and high level, and change strategies. If the user's main purpose for an interface is to search for information:

- ❑ *Plan for flexibility*. The user may want to search narrowly one time and broadly the next. They may want to start narrow and go broad or vice versa. Different users will have different preferred searching strategies. Users may want to save their own preferences to reuse.

❑ *Build in mechanisms to "go back."* Users may try a search and not like the result. Make it easy for them to go back and retry.

❑ *Plan for switching purposes.* After they search what will users want to do? Keep in mind that searching may be a temporary purpose. Users might be switching from search to another purpose. Does your interface allow them to quickly change gears?

❑ *Recognize human limits.* Don't overwhelm users with hundreds of items to search through. Provide filters to let them narrow further. Don't assume that they remember what they have searched on. Show them not only results but a summary of the criteria.

Browsing

Sometimes the user's main purpose at a given moment is to browse. This is a "window shopping" version of using a computer. They might be browsing through a tutorial, or browsing an online document, or browsing sites on the Internet. When users are browsing they want to wander at whim, switch direction quickly, or sometimes stay and linger for awhile. If the user's main purpose in using the interface is to wander through information:

❑ *Provide different layers of structure.* Provide high-level summaries that can be quickly scanned so that the user can decide if they want to browse deeper or keep moving.

❑ *Separate your purpose from theirs.* You may want them to stop and search, and stay and buy, but they may want to only pass through. Be respectful of their desire to get out quickly or they will just become annoyed and will not come back.

❑ *Grab their attention.* Use methods such as color, graphics, and corporate identity to grab their attention and draw them to what is critical. Don't overuse these techniques or they will become saturated and not pay attention to any one thing.

❑ *Make navigation easy.* Make sure that navigating through, in, and out of your interface is easy to learn and use. You want them to concentrate on content and not get frustrated over how to get in, out, and around.

Buying

When the user's purpose is to buy or place an order, for instance ordering a product from an online catalog, they are very focused. They may need to search or browse first, but you need to make sure they can easily complete the order. They expect the process to be as quick and easy as paying for an item at a checkout counter. If the user's purpose is to actually buy or place an order:

❑ *Allow them to switch purposes quickly.* Once the user has decided to make a purchase you need to stop selling. They are not browsing or searching anymore. They want a tool that makes it easy to place an order. After they order an item, make sure it is easy for them to switch back to browsing or searching in case they want to buy more.

❑ *Build in a quick and easy ordering process.* Make sure that it is very fast and easy to place an order. Do not require them to move back and forth between screens. When they are ready to order they should have all the information they need to complete the order, unless they change their minds.

❑ *Make it easy to change buying decisions.* Make sure it is easy for them to change their decision, for example, adding an item, or changing the quantity. Don't make them cancel the current order and start all over if they change their mind.

❑ *Follow "tool" guidelines.* Realize that once they start to place an order, they are actually using the computer as a tool. All of the comments above on designing a tool apply to good order forms.

Learning

Learning is a different experience than either a tool, browsing, searching, or buying. If users are using the computer as a learning tool, for instance taking a computer-based tutorial, they will need to have their attention caught and retained. This can be difficult if there are other distractions in the environment, such as telephones or other interruptions. If the user's purpose is to learn:

❏ *Keep their interest.* Use graphics, color, and animation to make the information interesting and keep them from getting distracted by their environment.

❏ *Use instructional design principles.* Learn about and use principles of instructional design to chunk information into meaningful bits. Don't overwhelm them with too much at once.

❏ *Minimize teacher talk.* Use boxes with text sparingly. People do not read large blocks of text on computer screens.

❏ *Build with easy in's and out's.* Make it easy for users to stop where they are and come back in later at the same place. Make it easy for them to start a small section over again without going back to the beginning.

Entertaining

Sometimes users are using a computer to be entertained, for example, playing a game. If the user's purpose is to be entertained:

❏ *Make the interface challenging.* Almost the opposite of a good tool, an interface for entertaining should be challenging and even difficult. The user needs to feel they always have something new to do, or a new challenge to overcome.

❏ *Watch out for assumptions.* Your idea of what is entertaining might be boring to someone else. Be specific in your assumptions and test them.

❏ *Pull out all the stops.* This is the time to use color, graphics, animation, sound, video, and so on.

About Guidelines

Part I of this book detailed the process of gathering and analyzing data, and creating usable designs. There comes a time in the design of an interface, however, that you must make concrete decisions about a particular screen, for instance, where to place a particular button, and what to name it. How can you ensure that you are making those correct detailed decisions? How can you ensure that all the developers on a project or across the enterprise are making correct decisions? The is the role of Part II of this book.

When standards and guidelines are followed during the design process, benefits for users include:

❑ *Reduced user's work time.* When applications are consistent in look and feel both within an application and from one application to another, users won't be distracted by the interface and will be able to get on with their work.

❑ *Reduced training time.* Users do not need to take time to learn the look and feel of each application.

❑ *Users become more involved in application design.* When guidelines are in place, and users know what to expect for the look and feel of the interface, they are better able to concentrate on the specific interface to get their job done, and give the most useful feedback to the design team.

When guidelines are used for design, benefits for developers include:

❑ *Reduced decision time.* If developers do not have to make decisions for each part of the interface, it frees them up to concentrate on one or more of the many other technical decisions they need to make.

❑ *Sound basis for decisions regarding users.* Rather than having to rely on the rationale "I just think it would be better," they can have the weight, research, and opinion of others with them through corporate guidelines.

❑ *Reduced programming time.* When guidelines include examples and templates, they can save time in programming, since developers are able to open and modify an existing template as needed.

Finally, two of the most overlooked benefits of using guidelines—items that benefit the entire enterprise—are the issues brought to the forefront, and the discussions that result from the work of multifunctional, multidisciplinary teams. The guidelines process gets players from different teams talking—talking not only about guidelines, but about projects, tools, challenges, and solutions.

Should you follow this book or customize? There are two ways to use the guidelines presented in this book. The first is to use it as is, either in hard copy or as an online document on the CD-ROM. The second way is to customize the text and pictures in the book for your particular needs.

Customizing the guidelines means working with the text and graphic files that are provided on the CD-ROM (in addition to the online version of the book). You can use the actual text and graphics, or edit them to create guidelines that best fit your needs, without having to start from scratch. There are many companies that used our first book (*Guidelines for Enterprise-Wide GUI Design*) in this way with much success. For more details on customizing the guidelines presented in this book, refer to the chapter "Best Practices for Customizing, Implementing, and Maintaining Guidelines," as well as the appendix "How to Use the Files on CD-ROM."

Structure

Contract Maintenance

File Edit View Help

New...	Ctrl+N
Open...	Ctrl+O
Close	
Save	Ctrl+S
Save As...	
Print Preview	
Print...	Ctrl+P
Exit	

Chapter 8

Contents

The structure of an interface refers to the windows, dialog boxes, and menus you use to create your interface.

Primary and Secondary Windows

Windows are the backgrounds that the rest of your interface controls sit on.

Use cascading windows

Cascading windows (see Figure 8.1) keep users focused on one task at a time. However, if by cascading you cover up information that needs to be viewed simultaneously, use tiling as shown in Figure 8.2

Tiling windows allows users to display multiple windows at one time without covering up other windows. However, the more windows the user opens, the more the windows shrink to accommodate the additional windows. Therefore information can also be hidden when using tiling.

Avoid horizontal scrolling

Avoid having users scroll horizontally to see information in a window or dialog box. Instead of horizontal scrolling, try one or more of the following:

- ❏ A larger window
- ❏ Breaking the information up into more than one window or using tabs
- ❏ Allow expanding, zooming in, and collapsing to show only some information at a time

Size secondary windows to fit data

Size secondary windows to best fit the information in them. Do not rely on users to resize windows, even if the window allows it. All secondary windows *do not* have to be the same size.

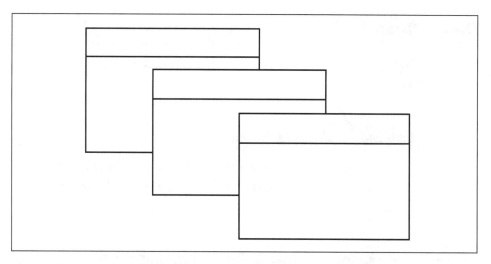

Figure 8.1 Cascading windows.

Place pop-up windows in the center of the action

Place pop-up windows and dialogs in the center of the area they relate to in the application window.

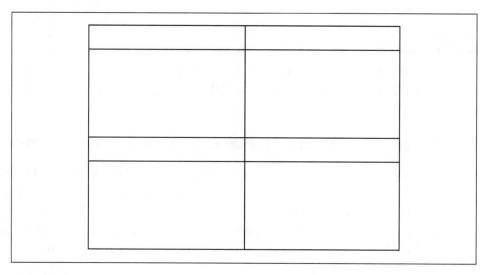

Figure 8.2 Tiled windows.

Dialog Boxes

Dialog boxes allow users to complete a set of actions for a particular task.

Use modal dialogs for closure

A user must respond to a modal dialog box before they can perform work in any other box or window. Use modal dialog boxes for form filling and small, discrete tasks.

Use modeless dialogs for continuing work

A modeless dialog box is a dialog that can remain open and active even while users perform work in other windows or dialogs. Use a modeless dialog box for tasks that need to be repeated or monitored over time, for displaying different objects at the same time, or when the user needs to have access to menus or toolbars while the dialog box is open.

Tabs

Tab cards are a popular conceptual model in recent graphical user interfaces. Tab cards can be useful, but they also have their drawbacks.

Consider tab cards for discrete categories of information

Tab cards are useful as long as users can tell by a brief title which tab would include a particular piece of information (see Figure 8.3). Avoid using tab cards when you have a lot of general information, where you may end up with a cluttered card or multiple cards with headings like Personal and More Personal. These titles are not discrete enough for the user to know where to look.

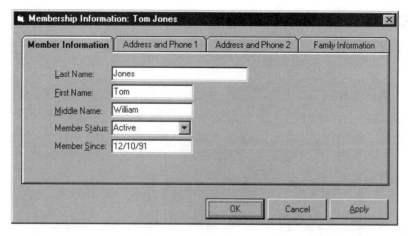

Figure 8.3 Don't split discrete information between two tabs. "Address and Phone 1" and "Address and Phone 2" are not discrete.

Tab card sets should relate to an object

A set of tab cards should relate to a specific object as shown in Figure 8.4. For example, one set of tab cards might contain information for a particular person, and include cards titled Address, Hobbies, and

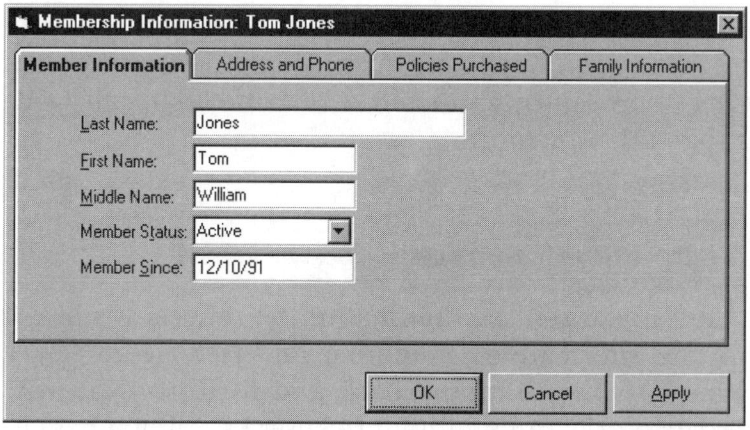

Figure 8.4 All tab cards relate to the object "Member."

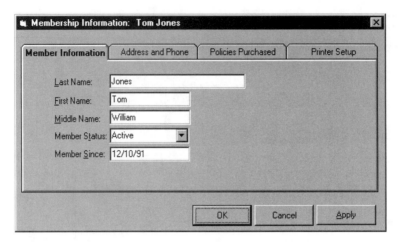

Figure 8.5 Don't mix objects within a tab card set. Tab card "Printer Setup" does not relate to object "Member."

Training. This set would have a person as its object. You would not have cards in this set titled Printer Setup or Defaults (see Figure 8.5). These cards might appear as a set for the Printer object.

Consider tab cards when the order of information varies

If the order in which information is viewed varies by user or by task, tab cards are a good way to organize information. However, if all users will view or use information in a certain order, tab cards may be slower than other methods.

Make sure the information is independent

Avoid tab cards when the information on one card is heavily dependent on the information on another card (see Figure 8.6). Users will either have to keep flipping back and forth, or you will have to change data on the cards without the user knowing it has changed.

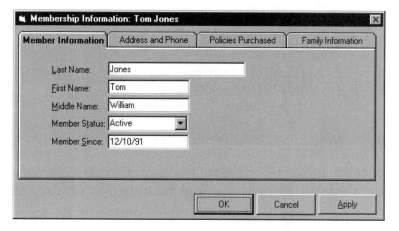

Figure 8.6 Information on each tab card is independent.

Use only one to two rows of tabs

Avoid tab cards if you have more than two rows of tabs—if you have that much information you need to consider a different method, such as menus going to forms or windows going to dialog boxes.

Use a master window or dialog box

A set of tab cards should reside on a window or dialog box (a "master") that also contains any buttons that affect the entire set of cards. Table 8.1 shows buttons that are commonly found on a master window.

Table 8.1 Buttons for a Tab Card and Master Window	
Button	**Action**
OK	Saves changes to any tab card in the set, closes the window
Cancel	Clears changes on any tab card in the set that were not invoked using Apply
Apply	Invokes changes made to any tab card in the set

Place buttons appropriately

If a button action pertains only to a specific tab card, place the button on the specific tab card. If a button action applies to the whole tab set, place the button on the master window.

Be consistent

Tab controls should be consistent within and across applications. If you use a master tab window and include OK, Cancel, and Apply buttons in one instance, you should use the same setup in the next instance.

Choose a horizontal or vertical flow

Decide whether you will use a horizontal or vertical flow of information for each tab card. Not every card in a set has to have the same flow—decide separately for each card.

A horizontal flow starts in the upper left and moves to the right. The most common or critical information appears in the top row. Less common or critical information appears in a second row. Buttons to control the window are on the top right. Use white space between rows to show the horizontal flow.

Vertical flow starts in the upper left and moves down. The most common or critical information appears in the left column. Less common or critical information appears in a second column. Buttons to control the window are centered on the bottom. Use white space between columns to show the vertical flow.

Menus

Menus play two critical roles in graphical user interfaces. They are a major form of navigation through the interface and they convey the mental model to the user in a snapshot. Giving attention to the design of usable menus is time well spent.

Word menu items carefully

Pick names and test them to ensure that they make sense to users. It is not easy to pick labels that users will understand.

Change menus as you need to

It is okay for menu bars and their drop-down menus to change as users move through an application.

Use initial capitals

Menu bar items should have an initial capital letter with the rest of the word in lower case. For drop-down menu items, follow book title capitalization rules—capitalize the first letter of all major words.

Follow industry standards for menus

Follow industry standards on menu bars and drop-down menus. You do not have to use these menu bar items or their drop-down menus if you do not have these tasks in your menu, but if you do use them, follow the standards. Figures 8.7 through 8.15 show the menus of different operating systems.

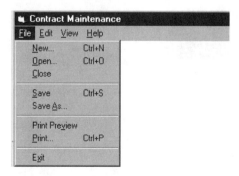

Figure 8.7 Windows 95 File menu.

Figure 8.8 Windows 95 Edit menu.

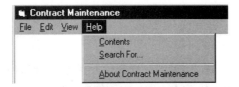

Figure 8.9 Windows 95 Help menu.

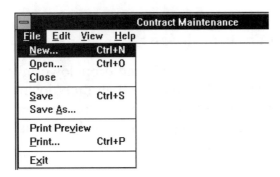

Figure 8.10 Windows 3.1 File menu.

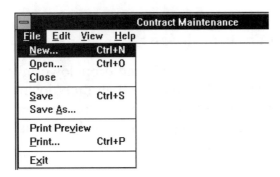

Figure 8.11 Windows 3.1 Edit menu

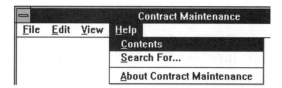

Figure 8.12 Windows 3.1 Help menu.

Figure 8.13 OS/2 File menu.

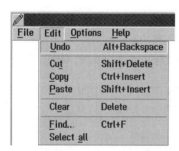

Figure 8.14 OS/2 Edit menu.

Figure 8.15 OS/2 Help menu.

Menu Bars

Menu bars point to major functionality in the application. Choose, organize, and name menu bar items carefully.

Match menu bars to the users' work flow

When users look at a menu bar it should match how they think of their work. Spend time deciding on and testing menu categories to make sure they fit the users' mental model.

Give critical or frequent tasks even weight

Make sure all critical or frequent tasks are represented equally on the menu bar. Avoid grouping all critical or frequent items under one category, and then using the remaining five or six items on the menu bar for different, but nonessential tasks.

Place application-specific menu items where they fit

Place menu bar items that are specific to your application where they best fit, for example, Jobs and Preferences before Help.

Use only one word for menu bar items

Items on the menu bar must be one word only. If they are more than one word, or use hyphens or dashes, it is hard to tell whether they are one item or two (Figure 8.16).

Figure 8.16 Don't use two words for menu bar items.

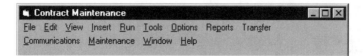

Figure 8.17 Don't use more than one line for the menu bar.

Use only one line for the menu bar

Menu bars must be only one line long. If you have too many items on your menu bar for one line, then collapse some of your items into one. The menu bar in Figure 8.17 is too long.

Do not gray out menu bar items

Do not use graying out to make menu bar items temporarily unavailable. Instead you should either not show the item at all or place the item on a drop-down menu where it is appropriate to use graying out.

Menu bar items should always activate a drop-down menu

Menu bar items should not initiate actions directly. Items on drop-down menus can initiate actions.

Drop-Down Menus

Drop-down menus reveal more detailed information to the user. Word and order them carefully.

Use more than one drop-down menu item

Drop-down menus should have more than one item on them. If you have a menu bar item that has one or no drop-down items, it should not be a separate menu bar category. Combine it with another menu item.

Figure 8.18 Don't start each drop-down menu item with the same word on the menu bar.

Use unique drop-down menu items

Do not start each drop-down item with the same word that is on the menu bar as shown in Figure 8.18. Drop-down items should be unique.

Limit drop-down menus to one screen in length

Drop-down menus can go from the top of the screen to the bottom of the screen. Do not use scrolling. If you have more items than will fit on the screen, you will need to combine some items and use cascading drop-downs, or separate some items into an additional menu bar item.

Put frequent or critical items at the top

Place the most frequent or critical items at the top of the drop-down menu.

Use separator bars

Use separator bars in two ways—to group related items (see Figure 8.19) and to separate destructive items.

Use no more than two levels of cascading

It is okay to use cascading drop-down menus, but do not use more than two levels of cascading. Figure 8.20 illustrates the use of too

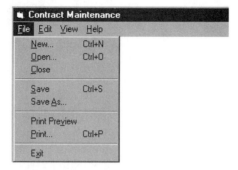

Figure 8.19 Separator bars used to group related items.

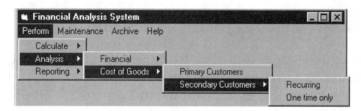

Figure 8.20 Don't use too many levels of cascading.

many levels of cascading. Use the right arrow symbol (▶) to the right of the drop-down menu item to denote that the item has a cascading menu.

Use ellipses (…) to denote dialogs

If more input is required to complete an action, use ellipses (…) after the drop-down item (see Figure 8.21).

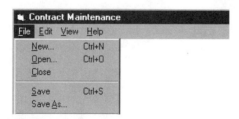

Figure 8.21 Ellipses after the "New" item indicate that more input is required.

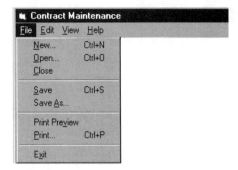

Figure 8.22 Keyboard equivalents show as underlined letters.

Use industry-standard keyboard equivalents

A keyboard equivalent allows users to choose a menu item without using the mouse. A keyboard equivalent requires that the drop-down menu be open when it is used as shown in Figure 8.22. All drop-down menu choices should have keyboard equivalents.

Use accelerators sparingly

Accelerators are combinations of keystrokes that allow users to choose a menu item when the drop-down menu is not open, as shown in Figure 8.23. Use accelerators only for those drop-down menu items that you think users will want to use without pulling down a menu, for example, Ctrl+V to paste from the clipboard. Figure 8.24 shows the standard Windows 95 Edit menu accelerators.

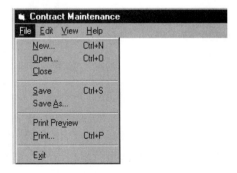

Figure 8.23 Accelerators show to the right of a drop-down menu item.

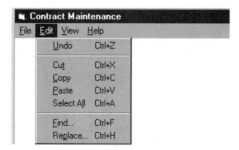

Figure 8.24 Windows 95 standard Edit menu accelerators.

Use consistent accelerators

Use consistent accelerators in your enterprise-wide applications. Place the accelerators in the drop-down menus to the right of the drop-down menu item.

Pop-Up Menus

Pop-up menus provide shortcuts for expert users.

Use pop-up menus for specific options

Pop-up menus appear when users click the right mouse button (see Figure 8.25). Use them for a subset of actions specific to the place or action. For example, if a user clicks the right mouse button on text in a word processing application, the pop-up menu would contain actions that could be taken on that text, such as Cut, Copy, Paste, and Formatting.

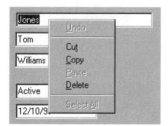

Figure 8.25 Pop-up menu.

Use redundant interactions

Don't make a pop-up menu the only place an action appears. Also provide a menu item, command button, or toolbar button for the action.

Roll-Up Menus

Roll-up menus can save space and are useful for expert users. Roll-up menus are floating, or movable, menus. They have a similar feel to toolbars. The user can activate them from a drop-down menu and place them anywhere in the workspace. By clicking the top right corner of the roll-up menu, the user can cause them to roll down (expand) or roll up (contract).

Use roll-up menus for frequent actions

Use roll-up menus for a group of actions that users will go back to frequently until they have the exact result they want, like applying special effects in a graphics application (see Figure 8.26 and 8.27).

Figure 8.26 Roll-up menu contracted.

Figure 8.27 Roll-up menu expanded.

Toolbars

Toolbars serve as a menu shortcut, or as a way to present controls that would be hard to convey in words, like drawing tools.

Make toolbars consistent

If you use a toolbar throughout the application, or between applications, make sure you use the same button graphics for the same functions throughout.

Make only active items available

Only toolbar items that are currently available should display. It is okay for some toolbar items to not show at all and for others to display as users move from one part of the application to another. It is all right for some items on a toolbar to be grayed out if they are only temporarily unavailable.

Allow users to move some toolbars

Allow users to move some toolbars to different locations on the screen to ensure they are out of the way of the work the users are performing.

Allow users to toggle toolbars on and off

Let users turn toolbars on and off through a dialog box or an option on a drop-down menu. This is especially important if you are providing more than one toolbar.

Allow customizing

Consider allowing users to customize their toolbars by deciding what to put on or take off the toolbar. You should, however, make decisions

Figure 8.28 Tooltip on a toolbar item.

on what should be on the toolbar and provide that as the default. Most of the time, users should not have to customize a toolbar for it to be usable.

Use buttons with a purpose

Pay attention to the number of buttons on a toolbar. Too many buttons create visual and cognitive strain. Users will not see some of the buttons if there are too many.

Use tooltips

If you have the ability to include tooltips (the label that appears as the mouse is delayed over a toolbar graphic) then include them (see Figure 8.28). Don't substitute tooltips for good design.

Group like items

If you have a lot of buttons on a toolbar, consider grouping them. For example, place all editing graphics together. Use white space to group them.

Relationship between Toolbars, Command Buttons, and Menus

You will need to decide which actions go in the menu system, which go on the toolbar, and/or which actions should be buttons on a window (see Table 8.2).

Table 8.2 Considerations for Proper Placement of Actions	
Action Type	*Proper Placement*
Most frequent and critical	Command buttons
Fairly frequent and across several screens	Toolbars
All actions: frequent, critical, and infrequent	Menu bar and drop-down menus

Use toolbars for frequent actions across screens

Toolbars should contain actions that users need to take frequently and need to access across several screens. Do not use toolbars instead of command buttons.

Use toolbars to supplement menus

Some toolbar items are used in conjunction with menu bars when users need a shortcut for certain actions. In these cases the toolbar items also appear on the menu bar.

Use toolbars in place of some menu items

Some toolbar items can be used in place of menu items. For instance, some drawing tools cannot be described with words and would be difficult to place on a drop-down menu.

Interaction

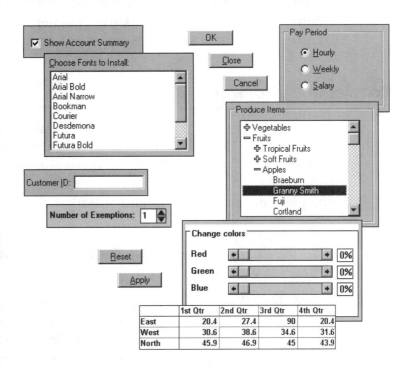

Contents

Interaction refers to the user's communication with the computer. The user and computer communicate through the use of various controls. Choosing a control is not just a matter of following a recipe. Selecting the right control means the designer needs to juggle industry standards, corporate standards, and user's needs.

Command Buttons

Command buttons are the primary way that users take action within dialog boxes. Use command buttons to convey to users the major actions of a particular box. Users should be able to glance at a dialog box and know what to do there and what to do next, based on the names and placement of the command buttons.

Use command buttons only for frequent or critical immediate actions

Use command buttons when users are going to take immediate action that is frequent or critical (see Figure 9.1). Command buttons act as reminders of what actions can and should be taken. Limit command buttons to a maximum of six on a window. Command button actions can also appear as menu items. If an action is not frequent and not critical, place it on a drop-down menu.

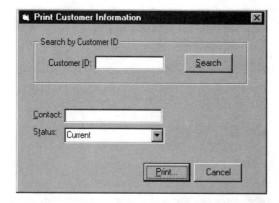

Figure 9.1 Command buttons are for frequent or critical actions.

Label buttons carefully

Make sure the label you use for a command button is clear and concise. For example, use Print Setup, not More. Use labels with multiple words when they are needed to clearly convey the meaning of the button, for example, use Print Current Orders, not Current. However, be concise and omit unnecessary words. Follow book title capitalization rules—capitalize the first letter of all major words.

Label buttons consistently

Choose specific labels for certain functions and use these labels throughout an application and from one application to another. For example, use List to display a table of choices, rather than sometimes List and sometimes Search.

Use industry standards for labels

Some labels have become standard across graphical user interfaces. Use these standard labels if you are performing the functions in Table 9.1.

Table 9.1 Standard Labels for Frequently Used Actions

Label	Action	Keyboard Equivalent
OK	Makes changes and closes the window	the Enter key
Cancel	Does not make changes and closes the window	the Escape key
Close	Closes the window when changes can't be made or canceled	C
Reset	Resets to defaults, leaves window open	R
Apply	Makes changes, leaves window open	A
Help	Opens online help	H

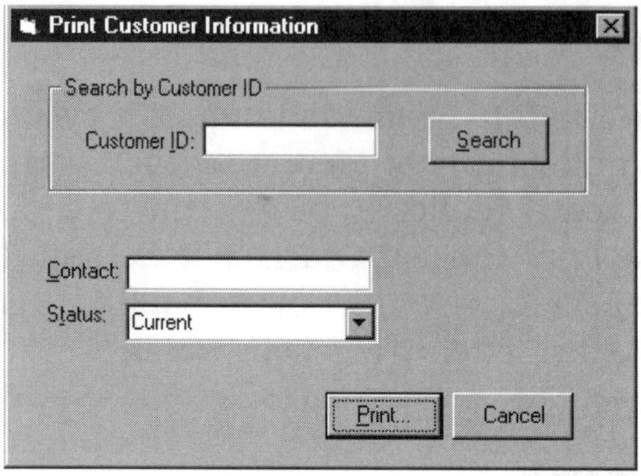

Figure 9.2 Print replaces a generic OK.

Consider replacing the OK button with a specific term

If the OK command button results in a specific function such as print-ing or deleting, consider using the specific term instead of the generic OK as shown in Figure 9.2.

Size buttons relative to each other

If the length of text for a series of command buttons in a dialog box is similar, make all the buttons in the dialog box the size of the largest button as shown in Figure 9.3.

If the text length for a series of command buttons in a dialog box varies, use two button sizes—one for shorter text and another for longer text, as shown in Figure 9.4. This allows you the button size

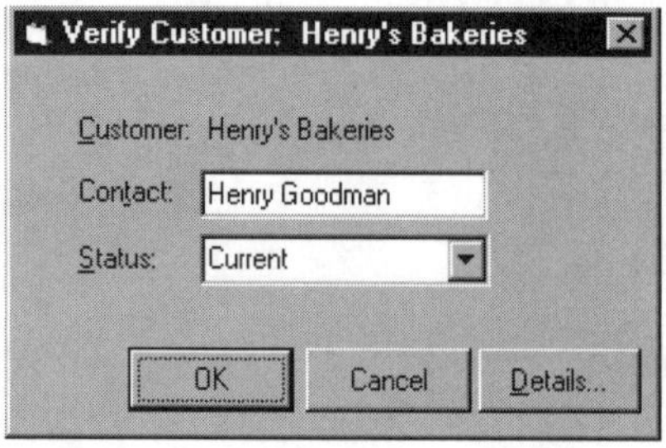

Figure 9.3 Buttons with similar length of text are the size of the largest button.

Figure 9.4 Current Orders is significantly longer than the other text of the other two buttons, so a different size button is used.

you need while avoiding too many different sizes. Do not use more than two different button sizes in a dialog box.

Separate buttons from the rest of the dialog box

Use white space to set off the buttons that pertain to the entire dialog box as shown in Figure 9.5. Don't crowd buttons with the rest of the controls in the dialog box, as shown in Figure 9.6.

Figure 9.5 White space is used to set off buttons for the dialog box.

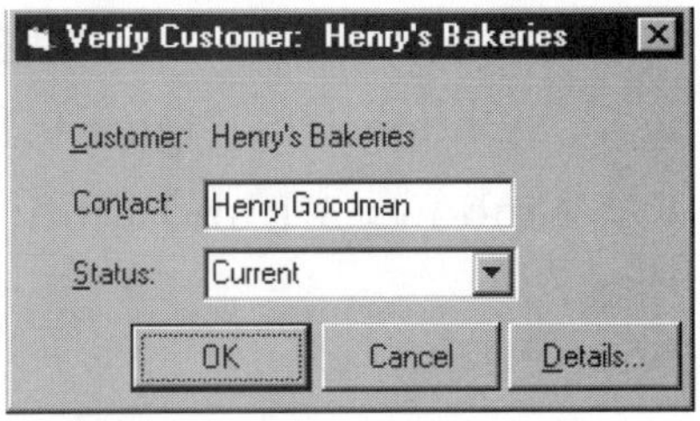

Figure 9.6 Don't crowd buttons with the rest of the controls in the dialog box.

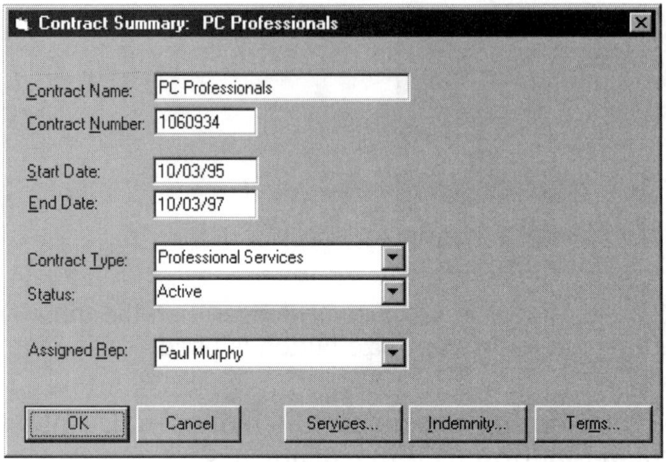

Figure 9.7 Buttons with similar functions grouped by using white space.

Group buttons together

If you have more than three buttons, use white space to group buttons together (see Figure 9.7). Group buttons to identify:

- ❏ Buttons with similar functions
- ❏ Buttons to leave the window (OK, Cancel)
- ❏ Destructive actions (Delete)

Place buttons consistently

Use one of these locations for buttons:

- ❏ Top right of the window (Figures 9.8, 9.9, 9.10, and 9.11)
- ❏ Bottom right of the window for Windows 95 (Figure 9.12)
- ❏ Centered on the bottom for Windows 3.1 and Motif (Figures 9.13 and 9.14)
- ❏ Bottom left for OS/2 (See Figure 9.15)

Do not place buttons in both bottom and right locations in one window.

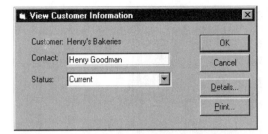

Figure 9.8 Windows 95 top right command buttons.

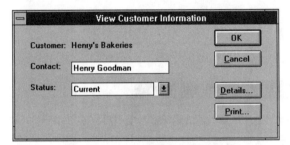

Figure 9.9 Windows 3.1 top right command buttons.

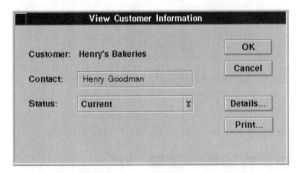

Figure 9.10 OS/2 top right command buttons.

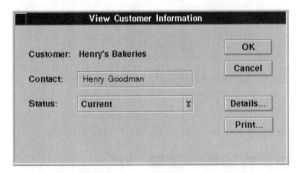

Figure 9.11 Motif top right command buttons.

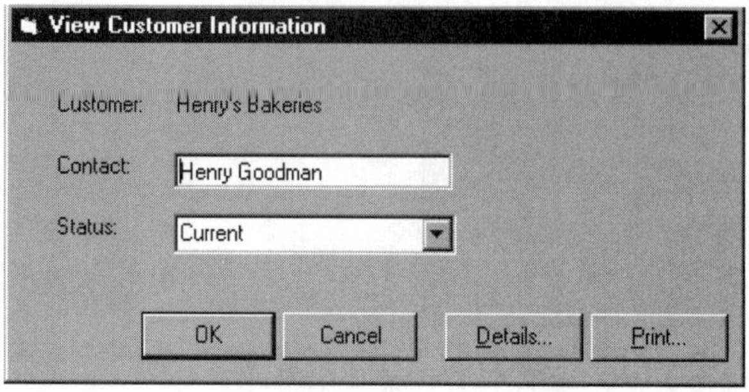

Figure 9.12 Windows 95 bottom right command buttons.

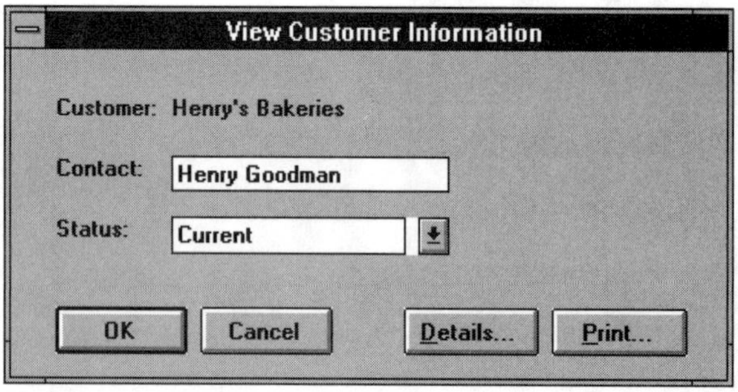

Figure 9.13 Windows 3.1 bottom centered command buttons.

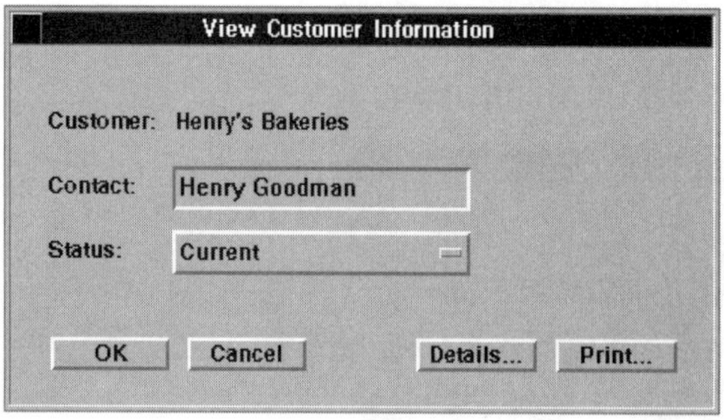

Figure 9.14 Motif bottom centered command buttons.

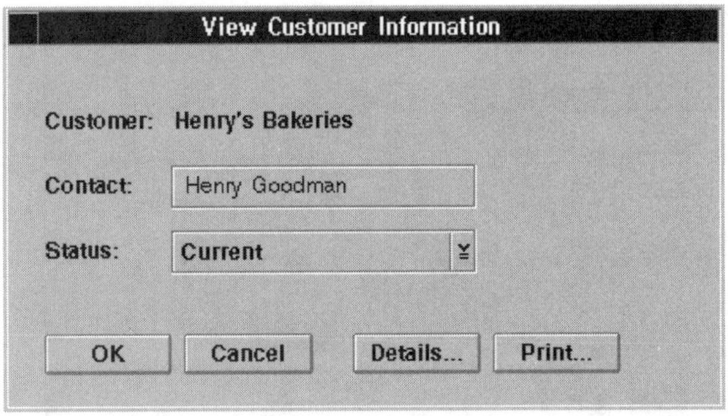

Figure 9.15 OS/2 bottom left command buttons.

Match button position to the use of the window

Choose either a vertical or a horizontal design for a particular window and position the buttons to match the design. A horizontal design should have buttons on the top right, as shown in Figure 9.16. A vertical design should have buttons on the bottom, as shown in Figure 9.17.

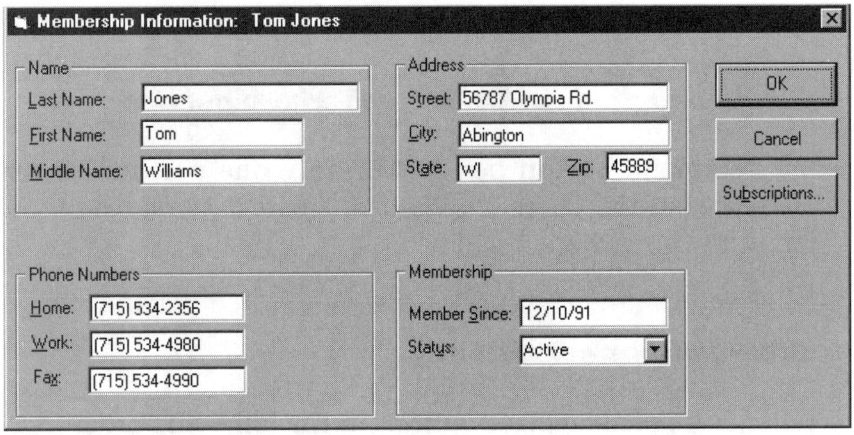

Figure 9.16 Horizontal flow command button placement for Windows 95.

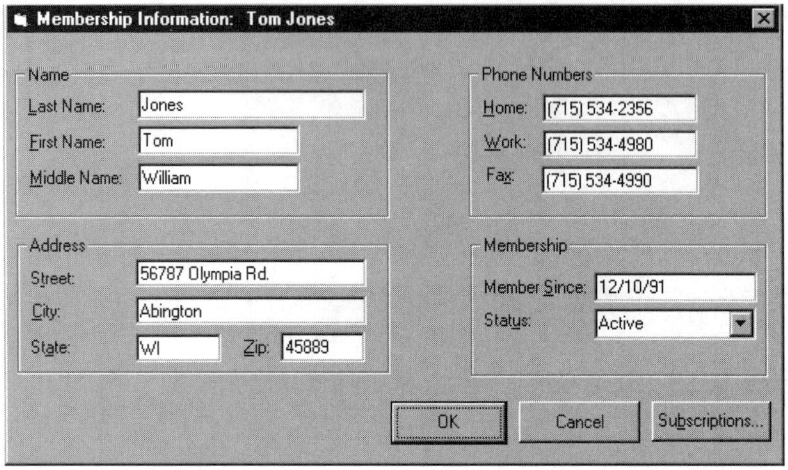

Figure 9.17 Vertical flow command button placement for Windows 95.

The grouping and layout of data in the window plays a role in determining which design to use. The length and number of buttons are also factors. If you have long button names or a lot of buttons, you may want to use a horizontal design with top right buttons. You can make these decisions on a window-by-window or box-by-box basis. Window flow designs do not need to be the same across all windows or boxes.

Position limited action buttons where needed

If a command button pertains to only one part of the dialog box, place the button where it is needed. Figure 9.18 places the Search button in the box where it will be used.

Order buttons consistently

Whenever possible, place buttons in the following order:

1. Affirmative buttons to leave the window (OK)

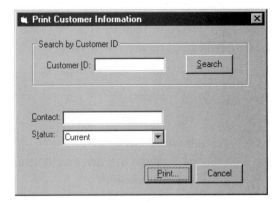

Figure 9.18 Search button placed in group box where it is used.

2. Canceling actions to leave the window (Cancel)
3. Unique buttons for the window

The order is the same for bottom or top right placement (see Figure 9.19).

Use ellipses (...) to indicate that input is needed

If more input is required to complete a button action, use ellipses (...) after the button name (see Figure 9.20).

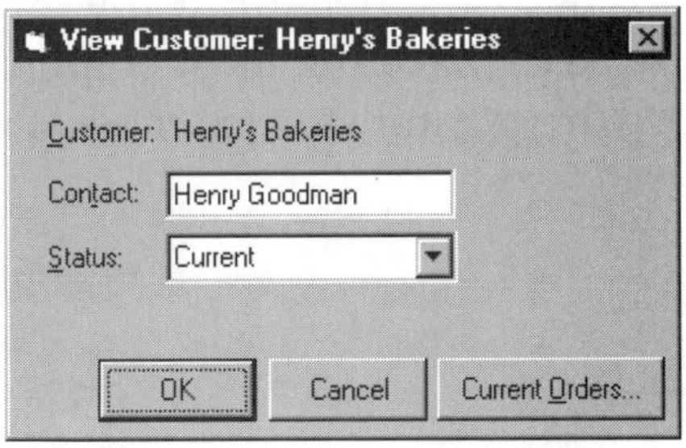

Figure 9.19 Affirmative button (OK) is first, followed by canceling action (Cancel), and then a unique button for the window (Current Orders).

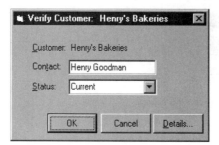

Figure 9.20 Another dialog box displays when the user selects Details, therefore ellipses are shown after the button name.

Gray out unavailable buttons

Use graying out to show that a button's action is not available. For instance, certain actions might not be available in order to restrict a user's actions until another step is taken. Figure 9.21 shows a Search button when the Search action is available. In Figure 9.22, the Search action is not available, so the button is grayed out.

Graying out implies that there is an action the user can take to make the button available. If in fact there is no action the user can take to change the button's state (the button will never be usable) do not include the button.

Assign a nondestructive default button

Choose one button on the window as the default. If the user presses the Enter key, that button is invoked. Make the most common or important action on that window the default, for example, Print on a

Figure 9.21 Search action available.

Figure 9.22 Search action not available.

print window. Do not use a destructive button, such as Delete, as a default, even if it is the most common or important action for the window.

Option Buttons

Option buttons, also known as radio buttons, replace many data entry actions.

Use option buttons for one choice

Use option buttons when users should pick one mutually exclusive choice from a list of options, for example, choosing a pay period in a personnel application.

Label option buttons descriptively

Pick a clear and descriptive label for each option button, for example, Send Course Description rather than Course.

Group option buttons together and label them

Place option buttons together in a group. Use a frame to show the group. Use a descriptive label for the entire group (see Figure 9.23).

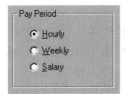

Figure 9.23 Option buttons grouped and labeled.

Figure 9.24 Align option buttons vertically.

Figure 9.25 Don't align option buttons horizontally.

Align option buttons vertically

Line up option buttons vertically (Figure 9.24), if you have the space, rather than horizontally (Figure 9.25) to make them easier to scan.

Limit option buttons to six or fewer

Limit option buttons to six or fewer choices. If you have more choices, consider using a list box instead. List boxes are discussed later in this chapter.

Choose an order

Decide on the best order for the option buttons. Some ordering methods include:

- ❑ By frequency—most frequently used options at the top
- ❑ By task—if there is a usual order in which parts of a task are performed
- ❑ By logic—if there is a logical order, for instance a list of dates
- ❑ By alphabet—only use alphabetical order if the labels match the way your users think about the items

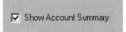

Figure 9.26 Use a check box for yes/no choices.

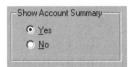

Figure 9.27 Don't use two option buttons for yes/no choices.

Avoid binary option buttons

If users need to make yes/no or on/off choices, use a single check box (Figure 9.26) rather than option buttons (Figure 9.27). However, use two option buttons for distinct, mutually exclusive choices, such as male/female.

Check Boxes

Check boxes replace some data entry actions and provide a quick way to make multiple choices.

Use check boxes for choosing more than one option

Use check boxes when users can choose one or more options.

Use check boxes for toggling

Use check boxes when users are toggling a feature on or off as shown in Figure 9.28. It is okay to have just one check box.

Figure 9.28 Use a check box for toggling a feature on or off.

Label check boxes descriptively

Pick a clear descriptive label that users will understand for each check box. For example, use Reverse Print Order, not Reverse.

Group and label check boxes

Place check boxes together in a group. Use a frame to show the group. Use a descriptive label for the entire group (see Figures 9.29 through 9.32).

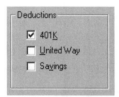

Figure 9.29 Windows 95 check boxes.

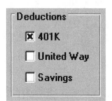

Figure 9.30 Windows 3.1 check boxes.

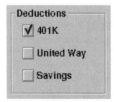

Figure 9.31 OS/2 check boxes.

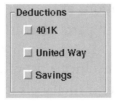

Figure 9.32 Motif check boxes.

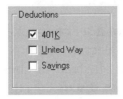

Figure 9.33 Align check boxes vertically.

Figure 9.34 Don't align check boxes horizontally.

Align check boxes vertically

Line up check boxes vertically (Figure 9.33) rather than horizontally (Figure 9.34) to make them easier to scan.

Limit check boxes to ten or fewer

Limit check boxes to ten or fewer choices. If you have more choices consider using a multiple select list box instead.

Choose an order

Decide on the best order for check boxes. Some ordering methods are:

❑ By frequency—most frequently used options at the top

❑ By task—if there is a usual order in which parts of a task are performed

❑ By logic—if there is a logical order, for instance a list of dates

❑ By alphabet—only use alphabetical order if the labels match the way your users think about the items

Do not use Select All or Deselect All check boxes

If you anticipate users will want to select all of a set of check boxes, or turn them all off, consider using a multiple selection list box with Select All and Deselect All buttons (Figure 9.35) instead of check boxes (Figure 9.36). Multiple selection list boxes are discussed later in this chapter.

Text Boxes

Text boxes are the main way for users to type in data.

Use a border to indicate data entry

Use a text box with a border to indicate that a user can enter or edit data, as shown in Figure 9.37.

Show display-only data without a box

If data is for display only and cannot be changed or added, do not place a border around it (see Figure 9.38).

Gray out temporarily protected fields

If a particular text box is temporarily protected, gray out the box and label to signify that data cannot be entered or changed at this time. Figure 9.39 shows a field in which data can be changed; Figure 9.40, one where it cannot.

Figure 9.35 Use multiple selection list boxes with Select All and Deselect All command buttons.

Figure 9.36 Don't use Select All and Deselect all check boxes.

Figure 9.37 Put a border around a text entry field.

Figure 9.38 Don't put a border around display-only data.

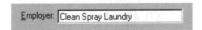

Figure 9.39 Data that can be changed.

Figure 9.40 Data that cannot be changed is temporarily grayed out.

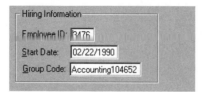

Figure 9.41 Each text box is a specific length to show the exact size of the field.

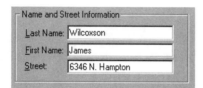

Figure 9.42 Text boxes are the same size if the data fields vary.

Use box length to signify approximate data length

Size text boxes to indicate the approximate length of the field as shown in Figure 9.41. If you have text boxes of similar length, make them the same length unless you need to show the exact size of the field. If the length of the field can vary, use text boxes of the same length to minimize the number of unique margins on the screen (Figure 9.42).

Align text boxes

Left align text boxes on the screen to minimize the number of different margins (see Figure 9.43). If a particular text box has a long label, use a different margin for that text box. Limit the number of unique margins to two.

Group text boxes

If you have text boxes that all pertain to similar information, group them together in a frame and label the entire group.

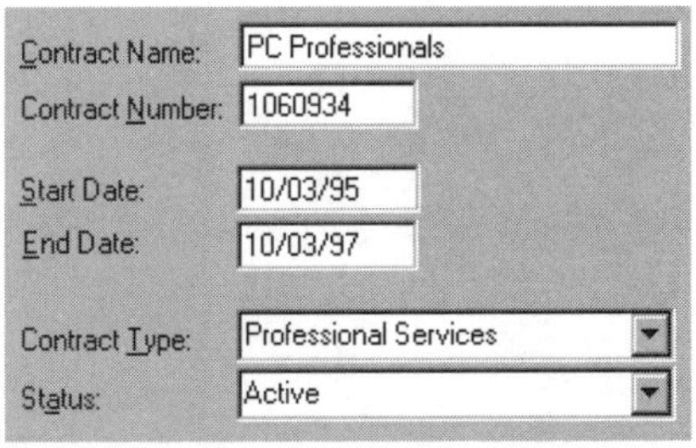

Figure 9.43 Text boxes are left aligned.

Label all text boxes

Assign a descriptive label to every text box. Avoid acronyms or abbreviations unless you are sure all users will understand them. It is okay to use multiple-word text box labels; however, keep them concise. Capitalize the first letter of the initial word of a label.

Place labels to the left

Place labels for text boxes to the left of the box. Avoid placing labels on top of text boxes.

Align text box labels to the left

Align text box labels on the left (Figure 9.44). Do not right-align labels. Right-aligned labels produce a ragged left margin, which is hard to scan (Figure 9.45).

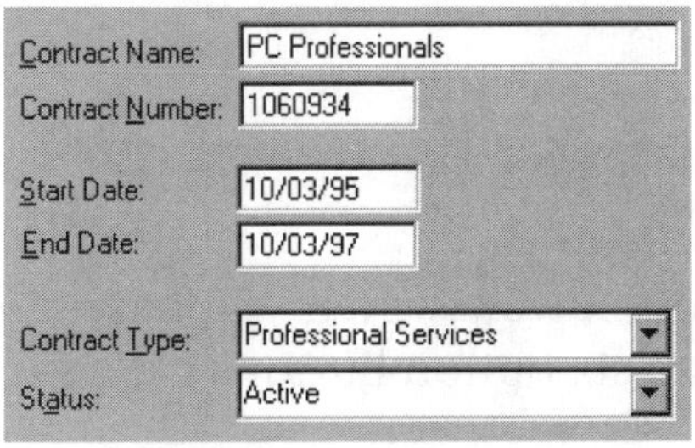

Figure 9.44 Left-align labels.

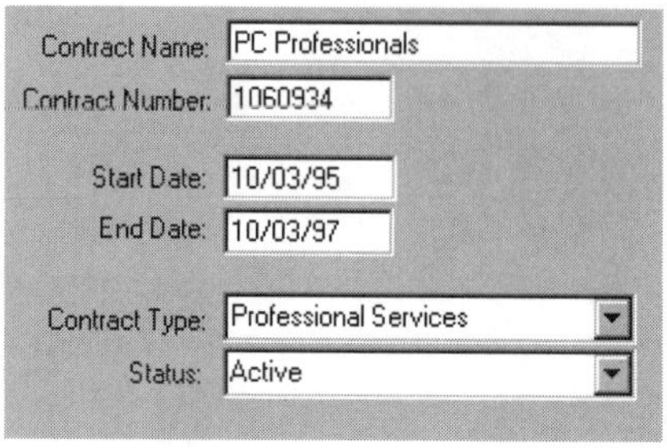

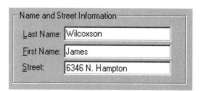

Figure 9.45 Don't used ragged left margins for labels.

Figure 9.46 Use colons after text box labels. Do not use colons after group labels.

Place a colon after text box labels

Use a colon after text box labels to distinguish between the label and the data that follows (see Figure 9.46). Do not use colons after group frame names or column headings.

List Boxes

List boxes are an alternative to long option button lists (Figures 9.47 through 9.50). They are also an alternative to data entry and they ensure data integrity.

Use list boxes for long lists

Use list boxes rather than option buttons when you have a lot of options. When you have more than six option buttons use a single selection list box.

Figure 9.47 Windows 95 list box.

Figure 9.48 Windows 3.1 list box.

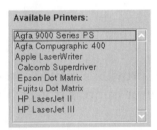

Figure 9.49 OS/2 list box.

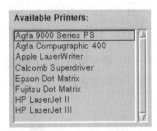

Figure 9.50 Motif list box.

Use list boxes for dynamic data

If data is likely to change over time, use a list box rather than option buttons or check boxes. It is easier to change the choices that appear in a list box.

Show three to eight items at a time

Show at least three, but no more than eight items in a list box at a time. If you have more items use a scroll bar to view the rest of the items. See the guidelines on drop-down list boxes later in this chapter.

Label each list box

Choose a label for the entire list box that describes the items inside the box, for example Available Printers. Place the label on the top of the list, left justified, followed by a colon.

Use filters for large lists

If there are more than 40 items in a list, provide a way for users to filter the list to narrow down the number of options from which they must choose, as shown in Figure 9.51.

Use drop-down list boxes to save space

Drop-down list boxes allow you to save window space. Use a drop-down list box if most users will select the first item. However, list boxes hide all but the first option from the users. Users have to go through an extra step to get to the rest of the list. Do not use a drop-down list box if it is important for users to see all the options all the time.

Use a combination list box to allow users to type in an option

A combination list box lets users type in a choice as well as pick it from the list. Use a combination list box when most users know what

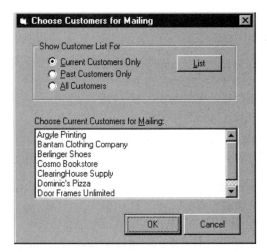

Figure 9.51 A filter is used for a long list of customers.

they want and prefer just typing it in. A combination list box is also useful when the list is long and users could skip down to a lower point in the list by typing in one or more letters. Do not allow users to add items to a list by using a combination list box.

Multiple Selection List Boxes

Multiple selection list boxes are an alternative to long check box lists. Multiple selection list boxes, however, can be hard for users to use. You may need to compensate for their usability problems by using the guidelines below.

Use a multiple selection list box instead of check boxes

Consider using a multiple selection list box instead of check boxes if you have more than ten options or your list is likely to change.

Consider instructions for multiple selection list boxes

Many users are not familiar with multiple selection list boxes. They might not know that they can choose more than one option or might

Figure 9.52 Instructions are included in label.

not know how to choose more than one option. Consider including a line of instruction or a prompt that tells users that they can choose more than one (see Figure 9.52). Instructions are particularly important when one window contains both a single selection list box and a multiple selection list box.

Consider a selection summary box

If you use a scrolling multiple selection list box, consider also displaying a box with a summary of what the user is selecting (see Figure 9.53). This way, the user does not have to continually move up and down the list to see what has already been chosen.

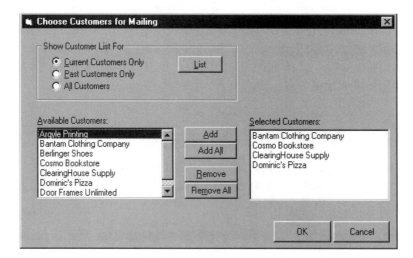

Figure 9.53 A selection summary box is used to display what the user has already selected.

Consider multiple selection checklists

Another way to show what the user is selecting is a multiple selection checklist. This combines a multiple selection list box with check boxes that the user can select.

Consider Select All or Deselect All buttons

If you have a set of options and anticipate that users will either want to select them all or turn them all off, consider using a multiple selection list box with Select All and Deselect All buttons, rather than check boxes.

Tables and Grids

Tables and grids allow users to enter or view larger amounts of information at a time.

Use tables for comparisons among data

Display a table if users need to compare two or three pieces of data and you can't predict ahead of time which they need (see Figure 9.54).

Use grids for multiple data entry

Use grids to allow users to enter several pieces of data at a time.

Label columns

Choose labels for columns that accurately reflect the data.

	1st Qtr	2nd Qtr	3rd Qtr	4th Qtr
East	20.4	27.4	90	20.4
West	30.6	38.6	34.6	31.6
North	45.9	46.9	45	43.9

Figure 9.54 Use tables for comparing data.

Use row labels if necessary

If rows contain different data, label each row.

Left justify labels

Left justify column and row labels. Do not use a colon after the label.

Spin Boxes

Spin boxes allow users an alternate way to enter data.

Use spin boxes for limited, predictable cycling

Use spin boxes to cycle through possible choices when the choice list is less than ten, as shown in Figure 9.55, and the order is predictable (such as days of the week).

Combine spin boxes with text boxes

If you use spin boxes, consider combining them with text boxes so that users can type in the specific value they want in addition to cycling through choices.

Sliders

Sliders are an effective way for users to quickly adjust values that do not need to be exact.

Use sliders for visually choosing values

Consider using a slider control to increase or decrease continuous values. They are especially effective if you show the result (see Figures 9.56 through 9.59).

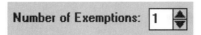

Figure 9.55 Spin box.

Figure 9.56 Windows 95 sliders.

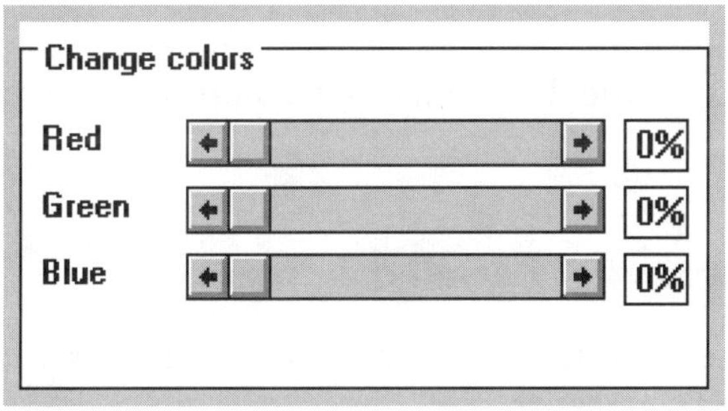

Figure 9.57 Windows 3.1 sliders.

Figure 9.58 OS/2 sliders.

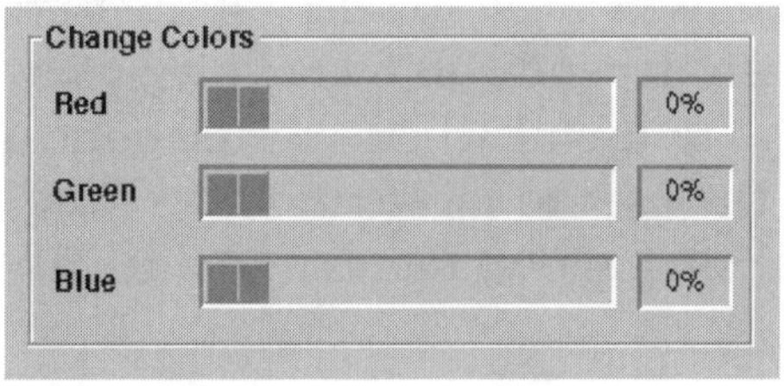

Figure 9.59 Motif sliders.

Use sliders for large data ranges

Do not use sliders for data choices fewer than ten. For small data ranges use a different control, for instance, a spin box or a text box for data entry. Spin boxes and text boxes are discussed earlier in this chapter.

Display results

Display the actual data value that the slider position represents.

Allow data entry

If users know the exact value, let them enter a value directly instead of using the slider.

Allow the use of arrows for small increments

Use arrows at either end of the slider for fine increments when users get close to the value they want.

Tree Views

Tree views show the relationship among items in a list.

Use tree views when hierarchy is important

A tree view displays the hierarchical relationship among elements (see Figure 9.60). It is useful when users need to select an item from a list, and the placement of the item depends on hierarchies, as in a file or directory system. Tree views are useful when the relationship of the item in the hierarchy helps the user to locate the item they are looking for. Expanding and collapsing allows the user to alter the amount of detail while they search.

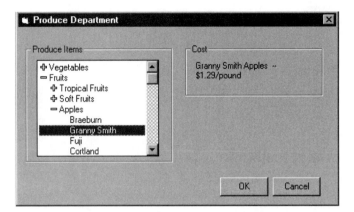

Figure 9.60 Tree views show hierarchy.

Use tree views for more advanced users

Many users are unfamiliar with tree views because they are relatively new and are not used in all programming environments. The tree view can be hard for users to use if they do not understand the relationships among the items, and may not realize the functionality of expanding and collapsing.

Do not use tree views to replace menus, home bases, or launch pads

Tree views should not be used to replace menu systems, home bases, or launch pads. They are useful as a searching and selecting control only.

Presentation

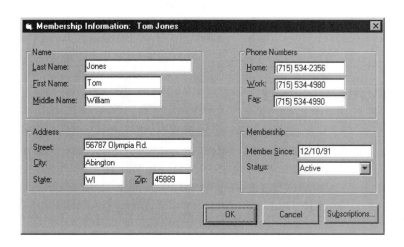

Contents

Presentation refers to how data is shown on screens and windows. Consider what the user needs to do with the data. Does the user need to compare bits of information? Does the user need to make selections based on certain criteria? Appropriate display of information can make a major difference in how useful the user perceives the interface to be.

Screen Layout

Screen layout principles have been with us for many years. Instead of becoming outdated, however, they have become even more important as more and more visual elements are added to screens. Make sure you follow the basics of good screen layout in your design. Users may decide that an entire application is unfriendly if the major screens are cluttered and hard to follow.

Organize windows and dialogs to match work flow

Which windows you have, how much they do, and the order they are in, should match how the users are doing their work.

Use an appropriate amount of information

Each window or dialog should represent one task or subtask in the user's work flow. If a task is complicated, use more than one window—one for each subtask.

Find a home base

A home base is the screen or window users come back to again and again while working on a particular task. Decide on a window that will serve as the user's home base. The home base might be a screen of data, a list, or a form with or without data. Home base is not necessarily the first window they see when they enter the application or a particular task. Users might go through a series of selection and list screens before reaching the home base.

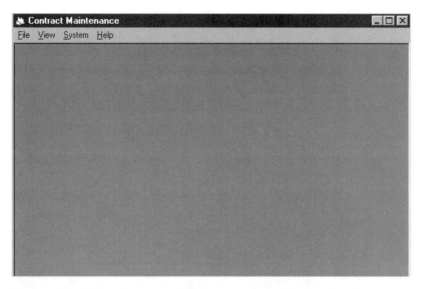

Figure 10.1 Don't use a blank screen as a home base.

Do not make home base a blank screen with a menu bar, as shown in Figures 10.1 and 10.2. It should be a screen with meaningful information for the task they are performing, for example, a list of con-

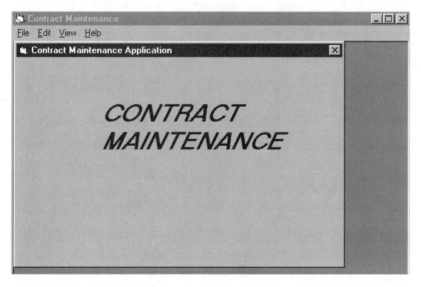

Figure 10.2 Don't use a blank form with a title as a home base.

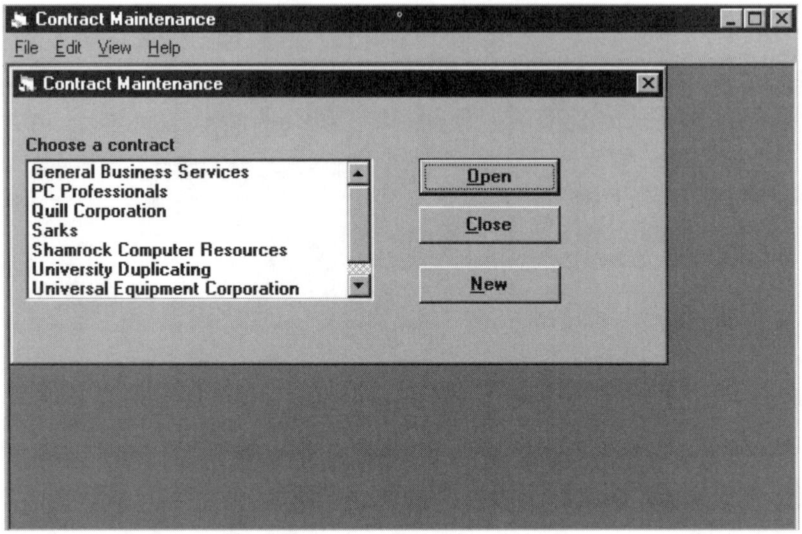

Figure 10.3 A list can be a home base.

tracts or a blank invoice form, ready to be filled in, as shown in Figures 10.3 and 10.4.

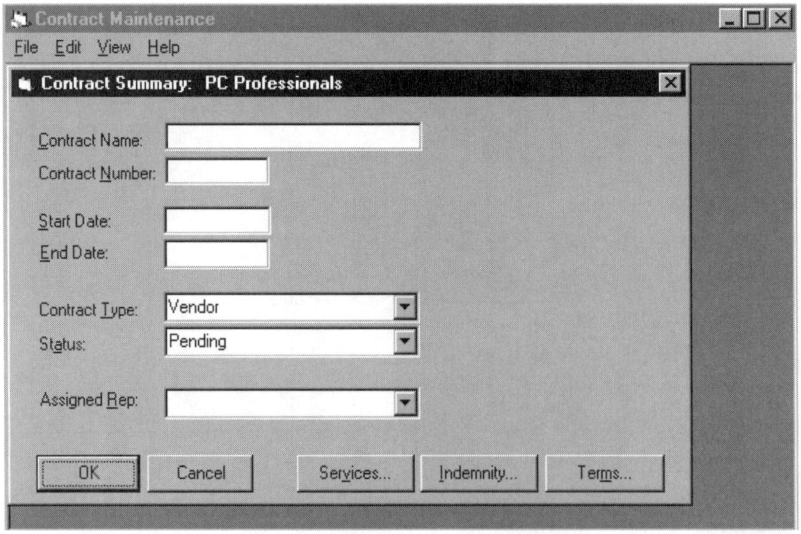

Figure 10.4 A blank form ready to be filled in can be a home base.

Having a home base helps users remember what to do, gives them a concrete and visual anchor point, and helps them to alleviate the feeling of being lost in the interface.

Organize information within a window

Information should be placed in a window or dialog box so that it flows well with the task the users have to perform. The most common or critical information should be at the top left of the window or dialog. The flow of the window should then move from top to bottom or left to right.

Choose a horizontal or vertical flow

Decide whether you will use a horizontal or vertical flow of information for each window or dialog. Not every window or dialog has to have the same flow—decide separately for each window or dialog box. However, do not use a mix of horizontal and vertical flows on one window or dialog box.

Figure 10.5 shows a horizontal flow that starts in the upper left and moves to the right. The most common or critical information appears in the top row. Less common or critical information appears in a

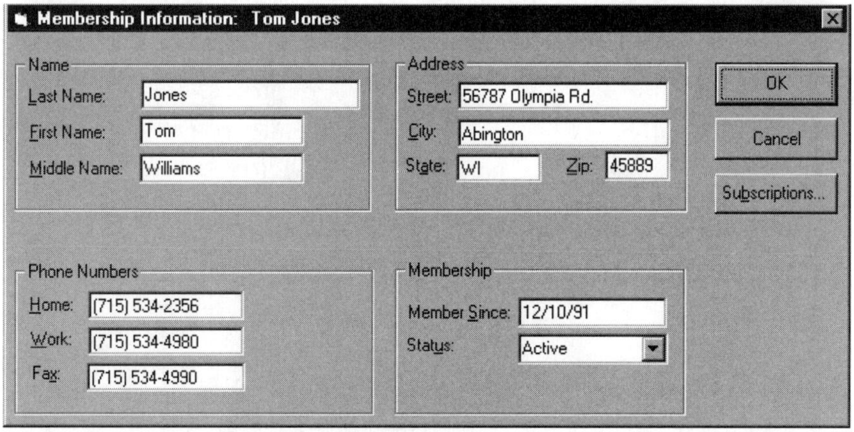

Figure 10.5 Windows 95 horizontal flow.

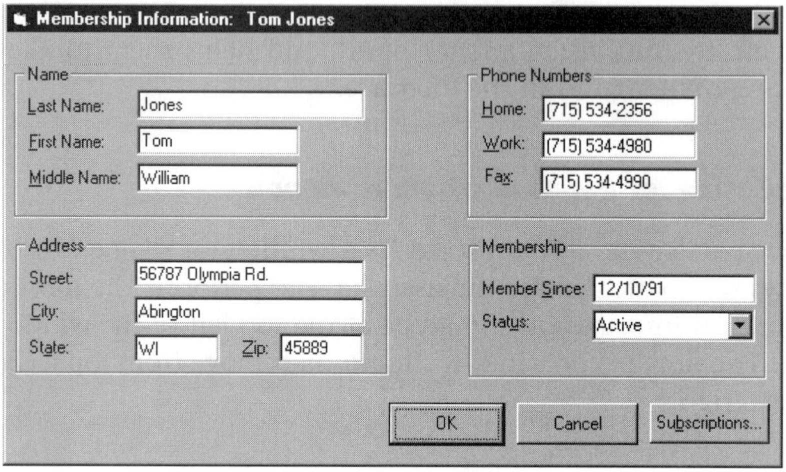

Figure 10.6 Windows 95 vertical flow.

second row. Buttons to control the window or dialog box are on the top right. Use white space between rows to show the horizontal flow.

Vertical flow starts in the upper left and moves down, as shown in Figures 10.6 and 10.7. The most common or critical information appears in the left column. Less common or critical information appears in a second column. Buttons to control the window or dialog box are

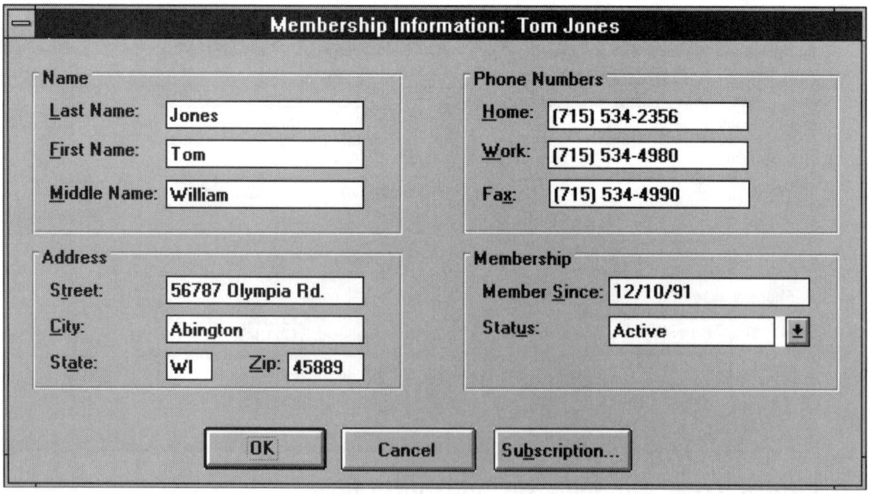

Figure 10.7 Windows 3.1 vertical flow.

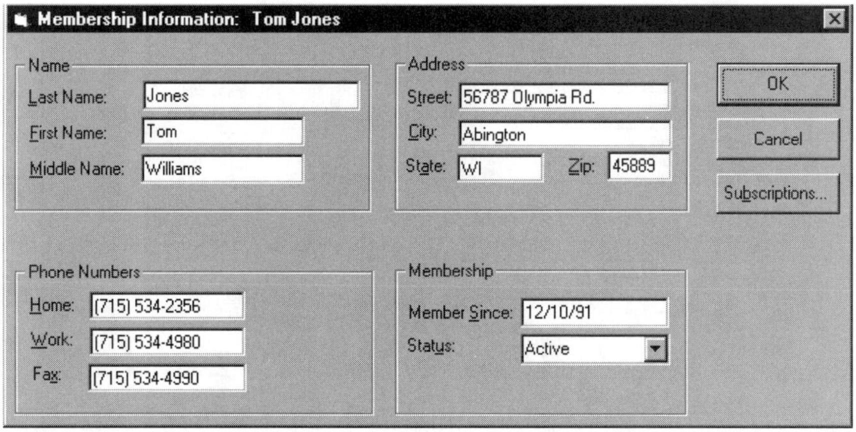

Figure 10.8 Similar data grouped.

centered on the bottom. Use white space between columns to show the vertical flow.

Group similar data

Group similar data together (see Figure 10.8). Use frames and white space to show the groupings. Label the groups.

Minimize different margins

Line up data elements and groups to minimize the number of different margins on the screen.

Fonts

With graphical user interfaces you have more choices in how to display text. This section summarizes good font decisions.

Use a sans serif font

Use a sans serif font for text and labels, as shown in Figure 10.9. Sans serif is easier to read on screen. Times New Roman is an example of a

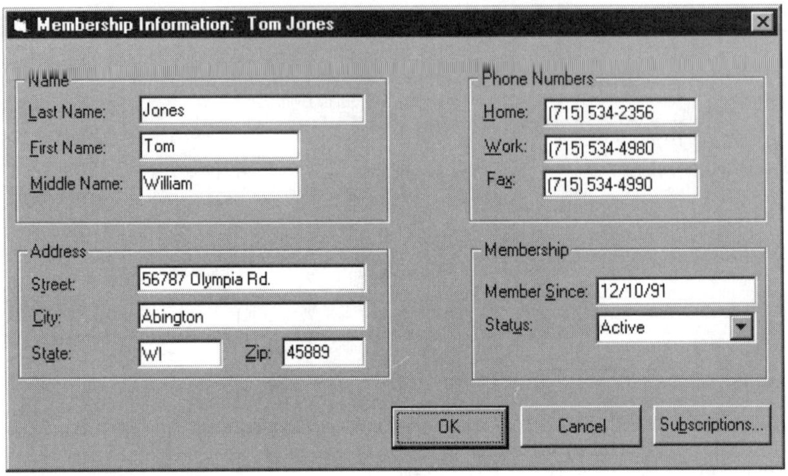

Figure 10.9 Use a sans serif font.

serif font (see Figure 10.10). It has "feet" on the letters. Arial is an example of a sans serif font. It does not have "feet" on the letters.

Do not use italics or underlining

Italics and underlining can make text hard to read on a screen.

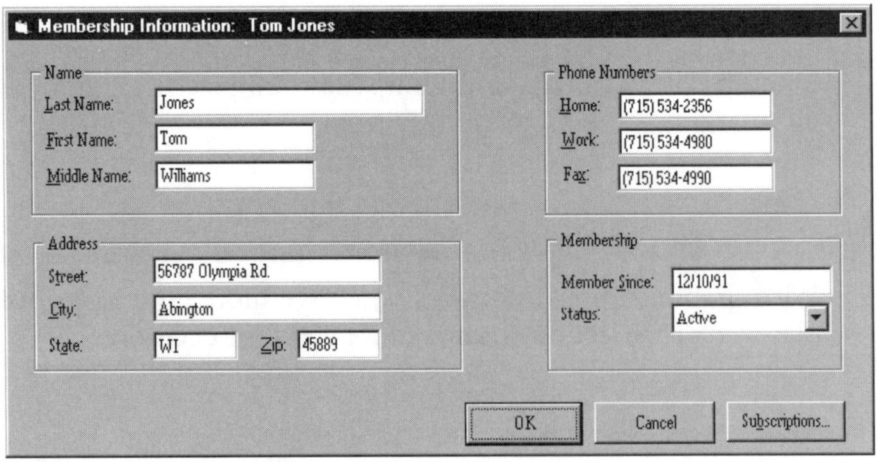

Figure 10.10 Don't use a serif font.

Avoid using colored fonts

The easiest type to read is black type on a white background. If you mix colors of fonts on one screen, the colored text will be harder to read than the black text. If you do use a colored font for a special purpose, consider bolding it to make it easier to read.

Use bold for emphasis

Use bolding to emphasize certain body text. Do not use color for emphasis because users typically assume color is a cue for text with a different or specific purpose, such as a label or a hypertext link.

Avoid changing font size

Avoid using font size to get attention. Many different font sizes on one screen can be distracting, as depicted in Figure 10.11.

Use at least an eight point font

Many people have a hard time seeing fonts less than eight points. An eight point sans serif font is the minimum for screen legibility, assum-

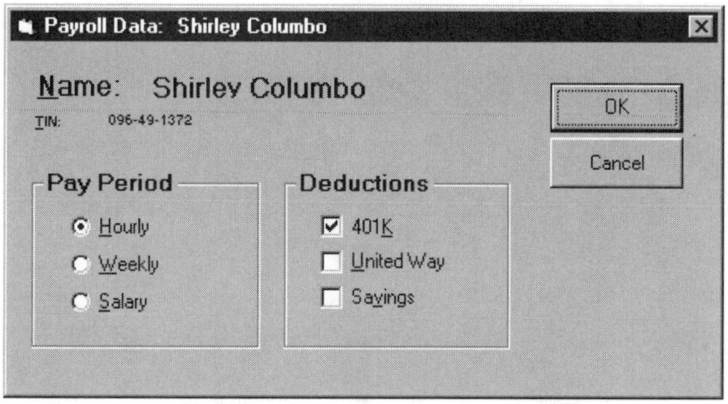

Figure 10.11 Don't use too many different font sizes.

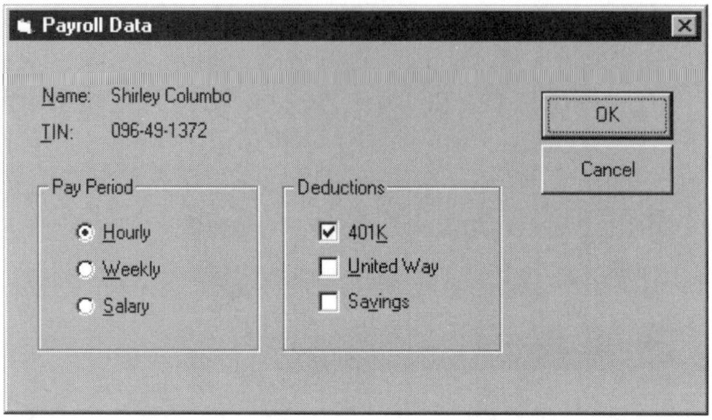

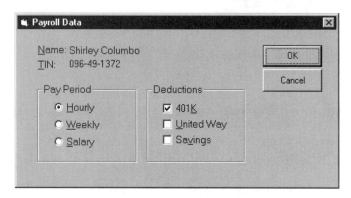

Figure 10.12 An eight point sans serif font.

ing a seated user at normal viewing distance. Compare the three font sizes used in Figures 10.12 through 10.14 for readability.

Figure 10.13 A ten point sans serif font.

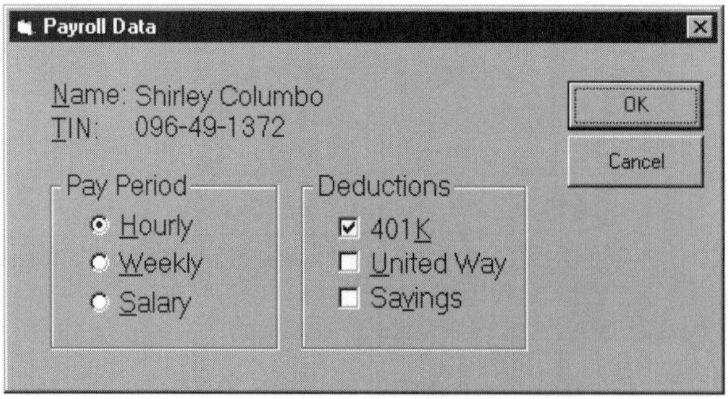

Figure 10.14 Don't use a twelve point sans serif font.

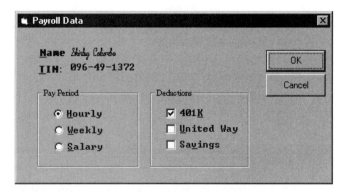

Figure 10.15 Don't use too many font types.

Minimize the number of different fonts

Limit the number of font types. Try to use one font type for all text. Figure 10.15 shows what happens when you use too many font types.

Color Choices and Combinations

You now have the capability of using color in your interfaces. Often, however, color decisions distract users rather than enhancing usability.

Use color to get attention

Putting something in a different color on a screen is attention getting. Use color when it is critical that users notice a certain part of the screen.

Use color purposefully

Color is a powerful attention-getting technique. Use it sparingly or it loses its effectiveness. Do not use it only for aesthetic purposes. Every time you use color it should be for a specific attention-getting reason.

Combine color with redundant highlighting

You cannot rely on users recognizing a particular color—for instance, some people have impaired color perception or can change their color palettes. Therefore, you should always combine color with redundant highlighting. For example, make a part of the screen blue and boxed.

Be aware of color blindness

Nine percent of men and two percent of women have some form of color blindness or color confusion. Do not rely on color alone to provide critical cues.

Watch out for color customizing

People can often change their color palettes. Do not refer to parts of the screen by specific color, for instance, "Enter data that is required into the green box." You cannot be sure that the box will always be green.

Use colors consistently

Decide on the specific meanings of colors within an application and use them and their redundant highlighting consistently.

Use color in toolbars sparingly

Because of their typically small size, using color in toolbar graphics is often more of a distraction than it is useful. Use color in toolbar graphics only to distinguish certain aspects of the graphic (different bars on a bar chart icon) or to establish a particular meaning (red in a stop sign).

Follow cultural color meanings

Be aware of the cultural meanings of colors for your particular users. In the United States, for example, some colors have particular meanings as shown in Table 10.1.

Table 10.1 Colors and Their Meanings in the United States	
Color	*Meaning*
Red	Danger, stop, hot, or financial loss
Yellow	Warning or caution
Green	Go or OK
Blue	Cool
Black	Financial profit

Do not violate these meanings and make sure you follow any additional meanings your users have. Be aware of international color associations—they vary from culture to culture.

Use light backgrounds for main areas

The best colors to use for screen and window backgrounds are off-whites and light grays. If you need to use a color other than these, use a pale yellow or pale blue.

Avoid red and blue combinations

Red and blue together, either as background/foreground or in adjacent areas, is very hard on the eyes. The combination of red and blue should be avoided.

Avoid blue text

Recent research shows that saturated blue text is hard to read. Use black text on a light screen.

Use enough contrast

Choose colors for your background and foreground that have enough contrast between them. For example, do not use a light blue background with medium blue text.

Avoid light text on dark

Avoid using light-colored text on a dark background. This combination appears to blur. It is better to use light-colored backgrounds with dark foregrounds. For example, use a light gray background with black text.

Use grayware first

Design in grayware first, adding color as needed. Use light colors for backgrounds and black for text. Although developers often consider this boring, it is best for users over the long run. Save color for when you really need to get someone's attention. Different shades of gray can be very effective in delineating areas on a screen.

Let users customize color

It is OK to let users customize the colors of an application, but do not use this as a reason for not choosing good color combinations. Users should not have to customize their screen appearance just because you picked poor colors.

Use color palettes

Provide a few color palette choices for users. This enables them to change all the colors quickly, and ensures that general principles for color use are not violated.

Provide a reset

If you let users customize colors make sure you have an obvious and easy way for them to return to the original (default) colors.

Consider showing results before setting

In some cases it may be beneficial to show users the results of their color decisions before they apply them. You can do this by providing a preview function with which they can see the color changes on a small sample screen before finishing the color dialog.

Designing or Choosing Graphics

Is a picture worth a thousand words? Only if it is well designed and well used. Here are some ways to make graphics powerful and effective.

Use graphics for a purpose

Decide how a graphic will be used before designing or choosing the graphic itself. Three common uses are:

❑ *Application icons*. These usually appear on the desktop. Clicking them launches the application.

❑ *Button images*. These are simple pictures that are placed on buttons, usually grouped together on a toolbar. Clicking them starts an action in the application, such as printing.

❑ *Descriptive graphics*. These graphics describe and support the user's task, for example, a picture of a house in a real estate application.

Use button images as shortcuts

Use graphics on command buttons when you want users to find critical or frequently used objects or actions without searching through menus.

Use graphics when a picture is worth . . .

Some ideas are best and most quickly portrayed with a picture rather than words, for instance, drawing tools or text justification commands.

Use graphics for international use

If you are designing for international and multilingual audiences, consider using graphics to eliminate the need to translate words. However, there are some guidelines to keep in mind when selecting graphics for international audiences:

- ❏ Make sure the graphics are widely understood. Test them with different groups.
- ❏ Do not use any offensive gestures. For example, a pointing finger is considered offensive in some cultures.
- ❏ Use representations that are universally held. For example, scales to show balancing are not a universal representation.

Decide on an approach

When designing a set of graphics you can use one of several different approaches. These are described in Table 10.2

Develop a cohesive set

Develop sets or families of graphics using the same approach described in the table above. Graphics for an entire application may involve several sets or families. Keep the number of different subsets to a minimum. For example, for editing a document you could use tools to represent actions such as scissors for cutting or a magnifying glass for enlarging.

Include just enough detail for recognition

If you are designing your own graphics, use just enough detail so that users can recognize the graphic. Avoid using too much detail or making the graphic look like a photograph.

Table 10.2 Examples of Different Icon Approaches

Approach	*Example of Approach*	*Example Graphics*
Object	A picture of a disk to represent an actual disk	
Action	A picture of someone running to indicate speed	
Tool representing action	A ruler to indicate measuring	
The result	Showing italicized text	*Result*
Physical analogy	Magnifying glass to show enlargement or zooming in	
Commonly used symbol	International "Don't Do" symbol	
Letter	The letter "i" for information	i

All pictures in this example are from *The Icon Book and Disk: Visual Symbols for Computer Systems and Documentation* by William Horton (John Wiley & sons, 1994).

Watch out for picture size

Often pictures that are easily identifiable when they are large become incomprehensible when they get turned into a smaller than postage stamp size picture on a toolbar.

Use standard graphics

If possible, use standard graphics that have already been tested. Check your platform's guidelines book and your programming tools for standard graphics.

Consider changing the graphic's state

Consider having a button image change to represent a new idea. For example, a closed file folder representing a file, which then changes to an open file folder representing an open file.

Be consistent

Once you have chosen or designed a graphic, use it consistently. For example, do not use different representations of a phone in different places in your application.

Avoid words

A well-designed button image should not need a label. If users can't decipher the pictures, you may need to fix the pictures rather than just adding words. If you do use labels, here are your placement choices:

- ❑ Use tooltips. If possible, have the tooltip appear when the cursor passes over the icon, as shown in Figure 10.16.
- ❑ Use a label underneath the picture.
- ❑ Use a label in microhelp (line at the bottom of the screen). Use this only if you cannot use either of the above choices.

Get appropriate help

Consider bringing in a graphic artist experienced in design for computer screens and the type of picture you need to create. People who

Figure 10.16 Tooltip.

are used to designing corporate brochures might not have the skill set and experience to create tiny pictures for toolbars.

Test your graphics

Make sure you test the graphics you design or choose. There are two basic ways to test:

- ❑ Give users a particular task and ask them to pick the graphic that they believe performs the task.
- ❑ Give users graphics in context and ask them what actions the graphics represent.

Charts and Graphs

Graphical user interfaces allow you to show data visually using charts and graphs.

Use graphs to show relationships

If you need to show relationships among different categories or over time, use graphs rather than tables with specific values, as shown in Figure 10.17. People can grasp trends faster from a graph than from interpreting data in a table.

Use bar graphs for categories

If you have discrete categories and are trying to show the relationship between them, use a bar graph. Bar graphs can also show multiple relationships between categories (see Figure 10.18).

Use special effects carefully

Use 3-D effects only if they help communicate the information. Avoid fancy formats if they don't help the user understand the data.

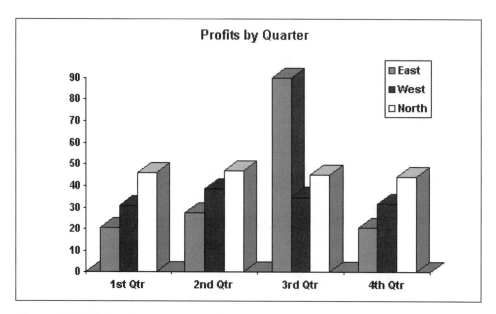

Figure 10.17 Graphs show trends.

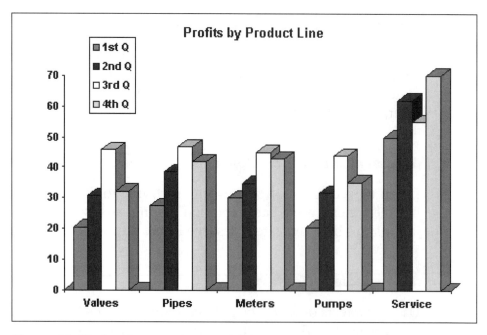

Figure 10.18 Graphs can show multiple relationships between categories.

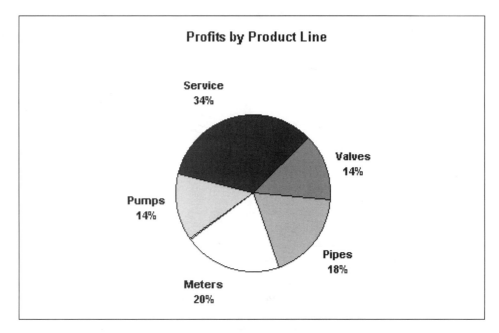

Figure 10.19 Pie charts show part-to-whole relationships.

Use pie charts for part-to-whole relationships

If you want to show part-to-whole relationships, use a pie chart, as shown in Figure 10.19.

Use line charts for continuous data

If you have continuous data, use a line chart rather than a pie or bar chart. A line chart better shows the cumulative effect (see Figure 10.20).

Choose appropriate scales

Choose an appropriate scale for both the X and Y axes of graphs. If the scale is too expanded, you may be exaggerating the effect. If the scale is too small, you may be underreporting the effect.

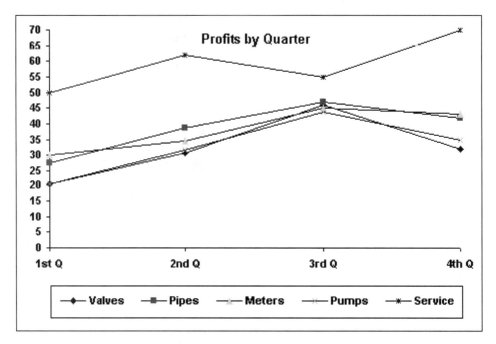

Figure 10.20 Line charts show cumulative effects.

Consider displaying specific values

If users need to see a specific value as well as a general trend or relationship, show the exact values on the graph itself.

Use visual coding on graphs

Use color, highlighting, shading, or patterns to distinguish parts of a graph.

Use legends for complicated graphs

If graphs have a lot of data and a lot of visual coding, use a legend, as shown in Figure 10.21.

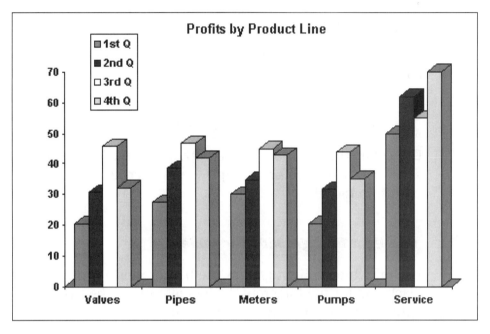

Figure 10.21 Legends help users understand graphs.

Label graphs and data

Label the graph with terminology users will understand. Consider the following labels:

- Graph title
- Lines, bars, or parts of the pie
- X axis
- Y axis

Use primary colors to show differences

Use primary colors like green, blue, and yellow in charts and graphs to make sharp distinctions. For example, use a different color for each bar in a bar chart, or each slice in a pie chart.

Use red cautiously

Avoid using red in a chart or graph unless you mean to imply trouble, danger, stop, or loss.

Use close colors to show transition

Use colors that are close to each other, like medium and light blue, to show a transition, for example, sales increasing step by step from month to month.

Use light backgrounds for tables

Use off white or light gray as the background for data in a table. Use black text for the foreground. Use color only when you need to highlight a particular cell, row, or column.

Use monochromatic backgrounds for graphs

If colors are used in graphs, use a white, gray, or black background.

Chapter 11

Internet and Intranet

A Wondrous Week of Fun and Excitement--1996

Contents

This chapter includes interface design principles that apply specifically to Internet and intranet applications. Designers need to know screen design and layout principles and how to incorporate the user's needs into site design.

Site Design

Before you start creating Web pages, there are some overall site decisions to make. This section covers general principles of Internet and intranet site design.

Provide meaningful content

Ask anyone what they want on the Web and they'll say, "Content." Be sure you provide accurate, current, substantive information. Content's value is determined by what the audience wants to know—not by what you want to say. Analyze your audience's interests before creating the site.

Give people a reason to bookmark your site

Supply information in the first page or two that makes people want to return.

Keep usability a high priority

Do not let your design get in the way of the functionality of your site. Be original and creative, but never forget usability.

Create a unified design

Use page design, repeated images, and colors to unify the pages in your entire site and in individual sections of your site.

Use a hierarchical structure

People think in hierarchies. Sites with obvious hierarchy are easy for visitors to understand.

Consider a grabber page

Some sites start with introductory pages that lead a visitor into the site and create interest before they arrive at the home page.

Use a home page as the menu for the rest of the site

A home page not only identifies the site, but it also provides entry into the rest of the site. It may do this with text links in lists or paragraphs, or it may do this with an image map or individual images. A home page must be strong. It must convince visitors to stay by letting them know what they will find.

Provide redundancy in home page menus

Be sure your home page is accessible to all visitors—from those using text-only browsers to those on the most advanced tools. Don't assume visitors will understand your image map or images without textual help.

Use submenus for large sites

The home page has links to major content areas of the site. If the site has a lot of categories of information and each category contains a lot of content, consider using submenus to help visitors navigate to the specific information they need.

Understand the bandwidths of your target audience

If you are creating an intranet site with high bandwidth lines, you can use multimedia and large graphics quite freely. If, however, visitors will be coming in on modems you must respect their needs by emphasizing loading time in your design.

Keep your file size small

Most advise that a given file be under 50 kilobytes—some suggest 30. If you assume that it takes a second to load a kilobyte, a file size of 50 kilobytes would take 50 seconds to load.

Provide a printing option for long pages

If you believe your visitors will want to print out a document to read offline, design your site so they can print a useful amount of information with one click.

Provide cues

Provide cues such as site maps, frames, and headings to keep your readers from feeling lost within your site.

Use a site map to indicate the relationships of information

Site maps are a means of indicating the size of a site and the relationships of the information within the site, as shown in Figure 11.1. They can be either graphical or text-based. Visitors can see the major information areas and understand that there are many links between the areas.

Make each item in a site map a link to the topic

Figure 11.2 shows how each item in a text-based site map should link to that page. If the site map is text, it loads quickly. Change link colors after they have been browsed so that visitors can easily see where they have been.

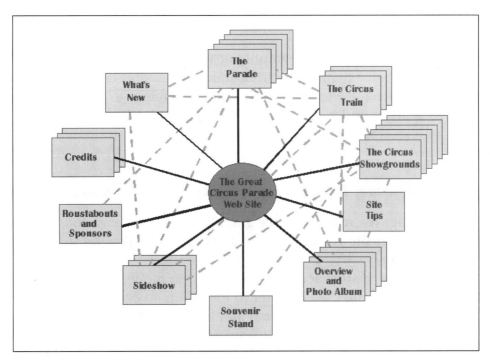

Figure 11.1 Site map from http://circus.compuware.com used as an image map. © Compuware Corporation

Figure 11.2 Part of a text-based site map from http://circus. compuware.com used as an image map. © Compuware Corporation

Use hierarchical text-based maps

Whether you use a graphic of the site or not, give visitors a familiar text-based map. This can be much like a table of contents, or it can resemble a tree or other form. Do not attempt to duplicate linked information under numerous headings—just include it once in its most logical spot.

Consider image maps for graphical navigation

Image maps are clickable graphics used for navigation. With a graphic of your site you can help visitors conceptualize the site and its organization.

For visitors accessing your site via modems, image maps (a single graphic) are usually faster to load than an equivalent set of individual images. However, this may not be true on fast intranet networks. Also, if the segments of the image map are used elsewhere on the site, it is better to use them as individual images because the browser caches them and then retrieves them from cache.

Image maps can be confusing for some visitors. Since an image map is often a complete picture in itself, it is often not obvious where to click. Until visitors have been on your site for awhile they may not associate a given image with content. Also, they may interpret the image, and its metaphor, as meaning something other than you did. However, an image map creatively designed for its target audience can be very effective. Figure 11.3 is on the home page of a corporation's site. The site provides information to employees on a new building and its neighborhood.

Prepare your pages for external search engines

Be aware of the confusion a visitor may feel. Search engines can bring a visitor into your site at any page. All hierarchical references are lost. Prepare for this by always having a link back to the home page and by

Figure 11.3 An example of an image map created by Ron Sova.
© Compuware Corporation 1996

telling the visitor the name of the site, and perhaps the area of the site, that this page belongs to.

Add a search engine to your site

As soon as your site grows to about 100 pages, you need to start thinking about adding a search engine, just for your site. This way a visitor can type in a few key words and then view a list of all the pages containing those words.

Design for multiple browsing environments

Refer to your audience analysis before using new technologies. Be sure your target audience is using advanced browsers before you create high-tech elements such as Java or floating frames. Always work with both lower and higher technology audiences in mind or many people will be unable to use your site, or be confused by references to functionality they cannot see.

Navigation

Navigation is important because if visitors can't find your information, they can't use it. And if they can't use it, they won't come back. Visitors must know they are at your site and must know where they are in the site.

Follow the three clicks rule

Design your site so that visitors do not need to click more than three times to get to the information they need. Details on the information might be deeper, but the basic information should be quickly accessible.

Use progressive disclosure

Use heading levels just like you do on paper—to indicate hierarchical information. Typically, your page title is heading one, main content categories are heading two, and a heading three is used if necessary. If you need more than three headings, you should consider linking to a new page for the finer detail. Those visitors interested in it can drill down to it. This process is called progressive disclosure.

Make navigation cues consistent

Keep all navigational elements the same on all pages—words and images—and keep them in the same place.

In a large site provide two levels of navigation

In a large site provide global, site-wide navigation from every page in addition to links within the subject area. For instance, in a corporate intranet you may always want the visitors to be able to get to Home, Search, the site map, and major content areas or departments.

Don't tie navigation or content to graphics alone

Those who either choose not to use graphics or who can't will miss critical content or not be able to use your site.

Provide text links to your pages

Return visitors have seen your graphics. What they want now is to get directly to the information they need. Avoid irritating them by making them wait for your images to load before they can use your site. Give them text links. These will come up first on the page and visitors can click on them without waiting for the entire page to load.

Use links carefully

Focus on the primary function of the page. Too many links (except on a menu page) confuse your visitors. Links within text disrupt the flow of the reading. Unless your text is clearly meant to perform a menu function, pull links out and list them elsewhere on the page. Consider placing all the links for a paragraph in a list at the end of the topic.

Make links to substantive content

Do not link to pages that are incomplete. Put the text in the source page, but don't create the hypertext link until the target page is complete. If you are linking to an external site, be sure that the link is significant to your audience.

Be sure the link text is clear

Links are the key to Internet documents. They allow visitors to decide where they want to go and what they want to read. They allow you to keep your files small, thereby making them quick to load. Write link text so that it clearly and accurately indicates the target content.

Make only a few words the active link

Linked text must be read quickly. Make only a few key words active.
  A poor example:

Placing links in a paragraph can make it easy to suggest the real content of that link, and the context in which you are recommending the link be followed.

A good example:

Placing links in a paragraph can make it easy to suggest the real content of that link, and the context in which you are recommending the link be followed.

Be careful with Previous, Back, Next, and Forward

These terms can be confusing to visitors. Do they mean the previous and next pages in a linear path through your site, or do they mean the previous and next pages in the order the visitor browsed your site? Your path and the visitor's path are probably not the same.
  Also, if you are using these terms to represent a linear movement through your site, remember that if you add or remove a section you have to recode these links on the pages preceding and following the page you have changed.

Avoid "Click Here"

Try to make your links a natural part of a sentence. Also, remember that the term "click" implies the use of a mouse. Some people may be using keyboard equivalents, not mice, to navigate.
  Do not say:

Click here to learn about links.

Say:

Links allow the visitor control over what they learn.

Avoid "Return to . . ."

Don't use phrasing that indicates a certain page order or flow. You do not know how a visitor came to the page, so do not assume that the word "return" is meaningful.

Be sure visitors can distinguish between visited and new links

If you do not use the standard link colors (magenta and blue), be sure that the colors you select for regular text and links—visited and unvisited—are different enough from each other that visitors are not confused.

Annotate all links to large files

Two forms of annotation are helpful. First, warn visitors about the size of any large file. Second, explain what they will find at the link if they take it (see Figure 11.4).

Use internal links for long pages

On a long page, place a list of links to content chunks at the top of the page. Visitors may not even be aware that they are linking within a document. They just know that these links are very fast.

Figure 11.4 Example of annotation on file size from http://circus.compuware.com/ © 1996, Compuware Corporation.

Maintain correct internal links

As you add to and delete from your site, your links may need to be revised. Be especially careful about adding and deleting pages if you use Next and Previous page buttons.

Bury external links

You probably don't want people leaving your site to follow an external link until they have really experienced what you are offering. Therefore don't put external links near the first part of the site. Bury them several layers in and down.

Check and correct external links frequently

Sites change location, cease to exist, or change their content. Check your links regularly and update them as needed.

Page Layout

Designing the layout of Internet and intranet screens is different from designing hardcopy layouts and from other computer applications. This section covers page layout principles specific for Internet and intranet applications.

Place the most important content at the top

 Very few people scroll below the information displayed on the page's initial screen so you must place what you really want them to see at the top of the page. Important links should also be at the top of the page.

Include standard page elements

Figure 11.5 shows the standard elements that every Web page should contain. These elements are:

❑ Page title in browser title bar
❑ Title of page
❑ Links to main topic areas in site
❑ Link to corporate identification
❑ Link to home, search, and site map
❑ Link to copyright page
❑ E-mail link to webmaster

Keep the home page on one screen

Display the important part of your home page on one browser screen, without scrolling, at 640 x 480 resolution, as shown in Figure 11.6.

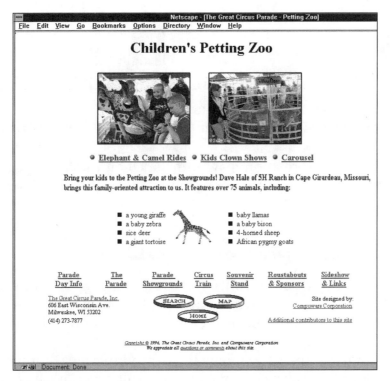

Figure 11.5 Page with standard elements from http://circus.compuware.com/ © 1996, Compuware Corporation.

Figure 11.6 Keep the home page to one screen.
http://www.ywcaogm.org/ © 1996, YWCA of Greater Milwaukee

Additional information may be included on the home page below the window break line if it is not important to the use of the site, as shown in Figure 11.7.

Pay attention to probable page breaks

Even though you cannot control much of the page layout, you must pay attention to where your pages will probably break—in other words, where the bottom of the browser's window will cut off the page when it loads.

If your pages appear to totally fit in the visible area, but they really extend down, it is likely that your visitors will never see the rest of the page. They will assume that what they see is all there is to the page. Arrange a text block or a graphic to extend below the break point so

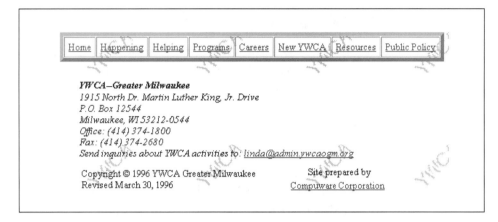

Figure 11.7 Place additional information below the window break line.
http://www.ywcaogm.org/ © 1996, YWCA of Greater Milwaukee

they will know they need to scroll. Test your layout on many different setups.

Decide on long pages versus short pages

Look at how visitors will use each page when you decide how long it should be. Long pages load more slowly than short pages. But if your visitors will need all the information and have slow modems, long pages probably load faster than many small pages (see Table 11.1).

Table 11.1 Determining Page Length	
If your visitors...	*Then you should...*
Want to find specific information quickly	Create many links to short pages
Need to understand an entire concept without interruption	Present the entire concept in one page with internal links to subtopics
Want to print all or most of the content to read offline	Use one long page or prepare a version that uses one page
Will be loading over slow modems but don't need all pages of information	Create a comprehensive contents page with links to many short pages

Break a long page up into smaller units

Use chunking and blocking writing techniques to break a page up into small units. Do this whether you leave the chunks in one long page or link to them as separate pages.

Use a grid

Use a grid to design each type of page on your site so that similar types of pages have a similar look and feel. Creating grids for page types during the planning phase of your project saves you development time and helps ensure consistency throughout the site.

Consider using tables

Tables are the best way available in HTML to control your page display. You can align objects and text, create vertical and horizontal space, and control the placement of images. Most browsers now support tables, however, you may still have to create nontable versions of your pages for visitors using text-only browsers.

Keep line lengths short

It is important to keep line lengths to no more than about two alphabets. This means two iterations of the lower case alphabet in the font style and size you have chosen. Remember that visitors can use any font style and size they desire.

Use tables to keep lines short

Tables, now understood by most graphical browsers, are one of the easiest ways to control line lengths. Use a fixed table width to keep the table from becoming wider when viewed on large displays. You can use blank columns to create white space or to hold graphics.

A drawback to tables is that text browsers cannot interpret them. For those using Lynx or other nontable-capable browsers, words and sentences in tables become jumbled. These visitors are not able to understand your information.

Consider using style sheets

If your browsers support style sheets, you have more control over page appearance. However, remember when you are using style sheets that you are designing for online, not paper.

Use enough white space

Only fill about 30 percent of your page with text. The rest of the space should be white space and graphics. Even if you use a lot of graphics, still leave enough open space to make your page comfortable and inviting.

Use enough horizontal spacing

Be sure to use enough horizontal space to allow your visitors to easily see logical groups of information, such as a chunk of text, its heading, and its related image.

Keep images and related text close to each other

One of the principles of design is proximity—visitors will assume a connection between objects, including text blocks, that are closer to each other than to other elements on the page. Therefore, place images close to their text and remember the reverse—if an image is close to text it will be assumed to relate to that text.

Use horizontal rules sparingly

Horizontal rules break up the flow of the page. Only use them when this is what you want to do, for instance, to separate standard header and footer information from page content, or to mark the beginning and end of a form.

Group the items in a form

Group related entry fields in the form and lay out the form so that it has a clear and logical flow.

Group long lists

Divide a long list of links into logical groups. Remember the "seven plus or minus two" rule—humans can only remember between five and nine items at a time—try not to exceed seven items in each group (see Figure 11.8).

Use hanging indents

Hanging indents are an important tool for Web designers. They allow clarity in separating list items, allow nested information, and help create additional white space. There are multiple ways of creating hang-

- **Background**
- How developed
- Purpose of the YWCA NET Program
- Lack of information about skilled trade careers

- **Challenges**
- Lack of role models
- Harassment and Discrimination Issues
- Lack of financial resources
- Lack of skills and experience
- Retention issues

- **Programs**
- Minority Apprentice Recruitment Program
- Transportation Allied for New Solutions (TrANS)
- CNC Machine Tool Training
- Model Road Construction Initiative
- Community Liaison Group top the OFCCP (with jump to Mission statement)
- Replication of the NET Program--Collaborative Development Process

Figure 11.8 Grouped list. © 1996, YWCA of Greater Milwaukee. www.ywcaogm.org

ing indents—tables, blockquotes, list tags, list tags without the list item tag, clear GIFs as spaceholders, and definition lists. For an example, see the grouped list in Figure 11.8.

Consider the design of bullets

If you use graphics for bullets, use an asterisk for the alternative text so that the image shows up as a bullet for nongraphical browsers. Use tables in order to be sure you retain a hanging indent, no matter what size of browser window or typeface a visitor may select.

Minimize vertical scrolling

Although this will depend on your audience and what they want from your page, research shows that people tend to lose interest if they have to scroll beyond three pages. If they are interested, they will seldom read this much online and will print it to read later.

Do not use horizontal scrolling

If Web visitors don't like vertical scrolling, you can be sure they will hate horizontal scrolling. Design for a 640 x 480 display setting and test. Be sure that tables and graphics fit in this area.

Page Titles and Headings

With all the Web pages in existence, paying attention to your titles and headings helps visitors notice and return to your specific location.

Make each title unique and meaningful

Be sure the titles that you choose accurately reflect the site name and the page content. Meaningful titles help prevent feelings of being lost or buried in your site.

Give each page a title

Each page needs a title that clearly explains the content of that particular page. These titles are usually coded in HTML as <H1> (heading one).

Use a name that labels the entire site and the specific page

In HTML a title code designates the text that displays in the title bar of the browser. Most search engines list the page title when they return the results of a query. It helps if visitors see the site name in this list rather than having to go to your page to read the headings. In addition, because visitors may come to your pages from anywhere, they need to know what site this particular page belongs to (see Figure 11.9).

Use headings to help visitors scan for information

Visitors want to quickly scan a page for the specific information they need. Help them by writing in small chunks and putting a label, or heading, before each chunk of text. Be sure these headings accurately reflect the content of the following text.

In long documents include document and chapter names on each page

To help visitors maintain their sense of location, indicate, in smaller text underneath the page title, what larger document the page is a part of.

Figure 11.9 Title bar includes site name and page name, from http://circus.compuware.com. © Compuware Corporation.

Frames and Windows

Frames are a method of dividing the screen into panels. Each frame area operates separately, so while one window scrolls, another can remain visible and stationary. You can create any number of frames, of almost any rectangular shape. Multiple windowing can also be provided by JavaScript. Frames are controversial. If you use them, be sure to subject them to extensive usability testing.

Use frames with caution

Many Web users find frames confusing. How frames work depends partly on the Web browser version the visitor is using. It may be hard for users to find the right scroll bar, and there may be too much scrolling required. Visitors may not know how to go back to a previous page. Printing can also be problematic. Visitors trying to place a bookmark will find that it only saves the site; frames don't allow visitors to bookmark an individual content page.

Do not use multiple windows unless they add functionality

Use secondary windows to add functionality to your site. Figure 11.10 shows how to use them for more detailed information, an illustration, or for a menu.

Limit the number of windows or frames to two

On a 640 x 480 monitor you have limited real estate. If you break the display area up into more than two windows or frames, you reduce the content viewing area too much. The visitor feels like they are looking through a peep hole.

Consider frames for global elements

All global elements, such as global navigation, corporate identification, and mail to links, can be placed on frames that remain no matter

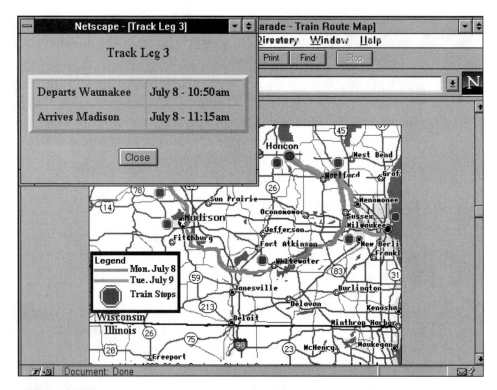

Figure 11.10 In this application, the reader clicks on any part of the train route map and the JavaScript secondary window opens giving information on that part of the route. © 1996, Compuware Corporation. http://circus. compuware.com/.

what content window is displayed. Content windows are freed from displaying this information. However, you should include some standard information on every page. If someone comes to your framed site from a search engine they view the pages without their accompanying frames. Provide a site name and a link to your home page so that these visitors will not be lost (see Figure 11.11).

Consider frames for pop-up text

You can design your frames so that a link from the main content page displays a small amount of pop-up text in a smaller frame, as shown in Figure 11.12.

Figure 11.11 The menu in the left frame is stationary. The content in the right frame changes with selections made on the left.

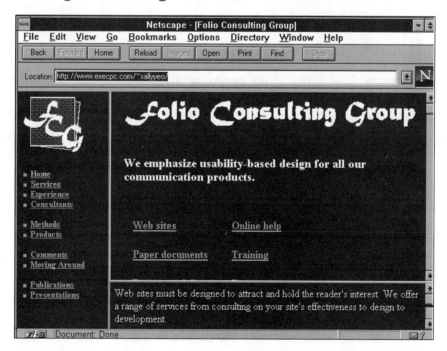

Figure 11.12 The lower right window changes as the reader clicks on options in the main window.

Use frames to keep lines short

If you design your site with frames, you can use them to keep text lines short in the main window of the site.

Watch out for window size

Many visitors complain that frames reduce the content window size too much. This is especially true when the designer has used more than two frame areas.

Graphics

Graphics, used correctly, not only enliven the text, but also make the intended meaning clearer. Graphics and text, when molded together, form a synergy—a whole that is greater than its parts.

Use graphics for a purpose

Graphics slow down your pages, so make sure they add value to the page. Never use them just because you think the page needs an image. However, people associate the Internet with fun as well as with content. Use this to your advantage by including images that make people enjoy your site. Pleasure is an important part of the Web experience.

Use text with graphics

Most graphics are not immediately clear to people, no matter how well designed. Add text to graphics used for navigation so that visitors do not have to guess where a click takes them. Use text to ensure that the graphics are communicating the intended meaning. If you omit text, conduct thorough and extensive usability tests.

Use alternative text

Many people browse the Web with graphics turned off, and a few people are still using text-only browsers. Use alternative text with all graphics so these people do not miss out on important elements of your pages, as shown in Figures 11.13 and 11.14.

Different browsers treat alternative text differently. Internet Explorer shows the visitor the graphic and the alternative text. The text appears just like the help text that displays when your cursor is over an icon in a Microsoft product. You can use this to add value to the image, as long as you don't put critical information in it.

Figure 11.13 Page with images on from http://circus.compuware.com/ © 1996, Compuware Corporation.

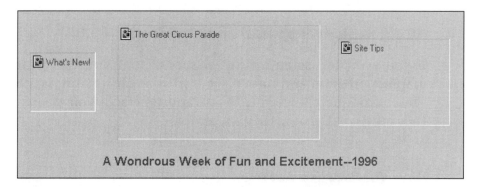

Figure 11.14 Page with images turned off © 1996, Compuware Corporation.

Netscape does not show the alternative text if the graphic is being displayed. You only see it if you have graphics turned off.

Nongraphical browsers display the alternative text in line with other text. If you are aiming your pages at this audience, phrase the alternative text so it flows well with your regular text.

Reuse images

When a browser loads an image it is saved on the local hard drive in a cache. When it is needed again it is recalled from the cache, eliminating another load.

Use images to help with navigation

Graphics can help visitors conceptualize the site and its organization.

Use graphics to represent content areas

You can use images to represent the major content areas of your site. Once visitors become familiar with your site they find the images faster to use than text. Be consistent and use the same images for the same content areas throughout the site (see Figure 11.15).

Use graphics for special headline fonts

If you want to use an artistic or special font you can create it in a graphics program and then place it in your file as a bitmapped image. This technique allows you to use any typefaces you desire, whether they are on the visitor's system or not.

Use graphics for lists

Provide some graphics to help visitors identify each group. A graphic clearly associated with the content of a list helps visitors quickly understand your organization scheme.

Figure 11.15 Key image used on home page as a menu item and on content page as an icon. http://www.ywcaogm.org/ © 1996, YWCA of Greater Milwaukee.

Remember the many limitations of images

Limitations such as 16-color monitors, low memory, restricted network bandwidths, color blindness, and poor vision affect the impact your images and backgrounds have on your audience.

Use thumbnails

Create a small version of an image (don't just rescale a large image in the HTML code). To keep the file size small, use the lowest quality GIF you can get away with. Link this small image to a large, high-quality version of the image. The small image loads quickly because it has a small file size. The visitor can choose whether or not to go to the large, higher quality image. Let the visitor know the size of the linked file (see Figure 11.16).

Size the image to fit on the screen

Remember that many visitors use a resolution of 640 x 480. In order to be sure that these people can see your graphic without horizontal scrolling, limit your image to 600 pixels across or less.

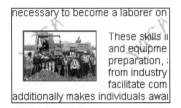

Figure 11.16 Thumbnail image linked to larger image from http://ywcaogm.org/ © 1996, YWCA of Greater Milwaukee.

Some browsers allow you to set the dimensions of an image as a percent of the browser window. For instance, you can say that you want the image to be 80 percent of the window width (leave the height unspecified). Test this in other browsers before implementing it.

Use as small an image as possible

Background patterns are images—GIFs or JPEG files. They can be slow to load. Make them as small as possible so they load quickly.

Simplify drawings

Drawings with minimal detail are easier to view online and they load quicker. If some visitors need more detail, offer them a link to a more detailed version of the image.

Use a low source image

Netscape supports an image tag that allows you to load a small image, such as a black and white version of your graphic first. Then it loads the color version. This tag is another way to give visitors quick results while loading a page. Browsers that do not understand the tag just ignore it. For JPEG images you can use a low-resolution version of the image as the low source and then have a high-resolution version come in over it.

Use interlaced GIFs

This technique allows images to start appearing in one-fourth of the normal time. The images are sent to the browser a few lines at a time so the visitor initially sees a very blurred image that gradually clears. This creates a page that feels like it is loading more quickly than if they had to wait for the entire image before seeing anything.

Don't put borders on the image in a drawing program

You can give an image borders via HTML code. These borders are supplied by the browser. Borders added in a drawing program add unnecessary size to the file.

Use transparent images over a patterned background

If you have an image that should float on the page, make its background transparent. For instance, a round image indicating a content area on your site will display as a round image inside a square box, because the bitmap is square. Make images like this transparent so they will float above the background. Test on different platforms and monitors.

Specify image dimensions in HTML

Browsers will calculate image placement by the Height and Width dimensions in the code and then quickly show the text on the page. The images will fill in as the visitor peruses the text.

Remember that search engines ignore images

Search engines do not find any text that is part of an image. Use alternative text and include the important words from image text in the HTML keyword meta tag so that search engines can find the page.

Backgrounds

Effective backgrounds add value to your site without distracting the visitor. Look for background patterns that support the message of the content.

Use light-colored backgrounds of low intensity

High-intensity colors, such as red, cyan, magenta, and bright green cause extreme eye fatigue when they must be viewed in large expanses for any length of time. White text on black backgrounds is also difficult to read. Reserve this for special effects or for pages that are primarily graphics.

Avoid patterned backgrounds

Patterned backgrounds can distract the visitor and interfere with the visitor's ability to read the text. Keep any patterns very light and conduct usability tests to make sure they do not make your pages difficult for your visitors.

Pick a random background pattern

Random patterns are more likely to tile smoothly across the screen. Nonrandom patterns often look tiled, which can be a distraction to your visitor.

Avoid watermarked text

Using text as a watermark pattern behind your content can seriously impact the readability of your pages. You can minimize this by spacing the watermarks out and placing them at an angle, but they still compete with the text for attention (see Figure 11.17).

transportation and budgeting, as well as assistance with industry awareness in the areas of tool usage, terminology and industry expectations.

The first year's training resulted in 45 individuals starting work. 34 of the group were African Americans, 5 were Native Americans, 13 were women, and one Hispanic.

An employers' "survey" "that   was developed to determine if the trainees were properly trained was administered in winter of 1995. The results indicated that all employers found an increase in applicant quality, as well as a higher rate of long-term retention.

The DOT renewed funding for a second year. There have been over 350 applications for the 60 training slots available. This training has been

Figure 11.17 Watermarked background competes with text. This example is from http://ywcaogm.org/ © 1996, YWCA of Greater MIlwaukee.

Use a background color when you use a background image

While the visitor is waiting for the background image to load, the background color fills the screen letting the visitor know that something is about to happen. Use a color that goes with your image so that the visitor is prepared, not surprised by, the image when it appears. Without a background color, changes you make to default text and link colors do not work.

Remember that visitors can set a default background color

Users can change the default background color with their browser to any color or background image they want. They may be able to choose to have their background override your document settings. Don't assume visitors are viewing the colors you chose.

Test backgrounds

Different monitors and platforms use different techniques for rendering color, so that backgrounds appear differently on different monitors and platforms. You must test your background on a variety of displays.

Color

Internet and intranet applications make liberal use of color. Make sure you are effectively using, not abusing, color.

Maintain high contrast

Black text on a white background has the most contrast and is the easiest to read. As you select colors with less contrast your text becomes harder to read.

Use large areas of uniform color

Large areas of the same color compress well and are an efficient use of the GIF format. Clean up solid backgrounds on scanned images so that they are a uniform color.

Reduce color depth

Reduce the number of colors in a GIF image to the lowest number you can and still retain acceptable quality. In many cases 50 colors give acceptable results. In JPEG images you cannot reduce the color depth, but you can try a low-quality version of the image and see if that is acceptable.

Use colors from the 216 supported by most browsers

Current browsers only support 256 colors, and most visitors use monitors set to 256 colors. Windows itself uses some of the colors, leaving only 216 actually available for Web images. Load the color cube (known as the CLUT, or color lookup table) from the Web and use this as the palette in your graphics program.

Use the same palette for all images on a page

Browsers load images faster, and the page size is smaller, if you use the same palette for all the images on a page. If the combined number of colors on your page exceeds 216, you may see some unexpected color substitutions in some of the images because the browser only has 216 colors to use for an entire page.

Avoid dithering except in photos

Dithering is a process in which the computer reduces colors by combining other colors to approximate the new color. Because of this blending of adjoining colors, dithering creates blurred text and line drawings and it makes it harder for the GIF process to compress the image. Reserve its use for photographs and continuous tone images.

Test colors

Different platforms and monitors use different techniques for rendering color, so that colors appear differently on different monitors and platforms. Test your color choices on a variety of displays. Also remember that some visitors are partially or completely colorblind. Take colorblindness into account when you make color choices.

Fonts

There are opportunities in Internet design to use different fonts. Follow these font guidelines to ensure your pages are readable and interesting.

Use sans serif fonts for online reading

The "little feet" on serif fonts, as well as other embellishments, are often lost onscreen because of the screen's relatively low resolution. Reserve using fancy fonts, designed for high-resolution paper printing, for headlines.

Use bold text for emphasis only

Bold text is a cue that something is more important than the surrounding text. If you bold all your text you lose this valuable cue. If you feel you need to bold text to make it stand out on a background, consider changing the background.

Use italics with care

Follow normal typographical standards for italics—use it for book titles and words used as words. Avoid italics for blocks of text because it is very difficult to read online.

Do not use underlining

Most browsers are set to automatically underline links. This is an important text attribute as it provides a cue to visitors who may be colorblind. If you use underlining with text that is not a link it may confuse a colorblind visitor. In addition, it is harder to read underlined text online.

Design for changes in font sizes

Web visitors can change the displayed typeface and its size. This can throw off your carefully aligned input fields and cause awkward breaks in field labels and instructions. Consider using tables with a fixed pixel width to set the alignment of a form so it won't be changed by different display fonts. You could also put the labels above the input boxes.

Use font tags to control text size

Use the font size tag to control the relative size of fonts on your page. Don't use heading levels to control text size because they are presented differently by different browsers—for instance, a heading six is very small in Netscape but very large in Mosaic. As style sheets become widely supported by browsers, learn how to control fonts using cascading style sheet codes.

Use fonts to express corporate identity

Fonts can express your corporate identity. Certain fonts create a modern, high-tech image, while others signify a more classic, traditional approach. The effect a font has on a visitor is hard to measure and is sometimes even subliminal. Choose fonts that help you create the image you want to portray, but coordinate fonts with content. Remember that your identity won't come across if the user can't (or won't) read your page.

Readability

Usability research shows that people don't like to read online, so you must make it easy for them. Reading online is much more difficult than reading from paper—glare from the screen, low resolution of fonts, longer line lengths, screen flicker, eye strain, and the relative lack of comfort are some of the reasons.

Write for visitor control

Understand that the Web visitor wants to control the reading experience. You must make it easy for them to read only what they want by making your writing concise and your main ideas easy to find. Give them links to pages with more detail. Do not force the detail on them.

Say it once, quickly

People don't like to read online. Make sure your sentences are direct and short. Eliminate all redundancy and paragraph transitions. Eliminate all unnecessary words and phrases. Use bulleted lists. Write for quick comprehension.

Design for scanning

Online visitors scan for the information they need. Visitors use headings, graphics, and colored or bolded text to find what they need.

Write in short chunks

Write in short chunks of no more than four or five sentences. Visually these chunks (paragraphs) should give the feeling of being short and to the point. Include only one topic in each chunk and make sure that no extraneous sentences sneak in.

Create clear concise labels for text chunks

Make sure that each heading, or label, for each chunk is short and clear. It must accurately represent the content of that chunk.

Use an active writing style

Write directly to your visitors by using the second person. Use the present tense—it is shorter and more direct. Avoid the passive voice. The active voice creates shorter sentences, is easier to comprehend quickly, and names responsibility.

Write positive messages

Write all your messages in the affirmative. Be nonjudgmental and be sure the message includes constructive information on what the visitor needs to do.

Use normal writing conventions for lists

Follow normal writing conventions when using lists. Keep phrasing consistent—have all items in a list sentences or phrases, but don't mix them. Be consistent in punctuation and capitalization.

Netiquette

There are certain principles of etiquette that designers should follow when working on the Web.

Keep information current

Keep content current, and let visitors know what is new or updated. A common way of doing this is to have a "What's New" page or to put New icons next to new information on existing pages.

Put a "Last Updated" date in your footer

Currency of information on the Web is critical. Because the ability to keep information up to date is one of the web's primary attractions, it is also an expectation of your visitors. Let them know when you last updated the information.

Give visitors something to do while they wait

If you provide enough text on your site to hold their interest, visitors will be more patient while your images load. Having text links appear quickly also helps visitors use your site.

Don't use other's material or code without permission and credit

Although copyright law for the Internet is still under development, we should all remember to use common courtesy, basic ethics, and the established practices of paper copyright. If you can see it on the Web, it is copyrighted unless the creator of the object has specifically said it is free for everyone's use. If you use someone else's work, ask permission and give credit.

Provide a way for visitors to talk back to you

Provide either a response form or a way for visitors to send you email. People want to tell you things about your site. Be sure to capitalize on this valuable feedback. Visitor feedback can give you excellent clues about what needs changing—navigation problems, slow-loading pages, and inaccurate or old content are just a few of the elements people communicate to you.

Answer your mail

If people send you mail, answer it if at all possible.

Ask permission before linking to someone's site

It is common courtesy to ask permission before linking to someone's site. They will probably be glad for the link, but it is possible they may refuse if they feel your site is too different in style or content from theirs.

Get permission to use trademarks and logos

Be very careful about using trademarks, logos, and trademark-type images. Corporations closely guard them and prosecute if you use them incorrectly. Get permission first.

Indicate that your information is copyrighted

It is best to remind your visitors that your information, images, and code are yours, not theirs for the taking. Create a copyright page and link to it from your other pages.

Be careful about humor

Be very careful in your use of humor. Most humor is very culturally dependent. People from other cultures may either be offended or not understand it.

Consider the needs of disabled visitors

Many people with physical challenges spend a great deal of time on the Internet. Even though they may form a small part of your potential audience, you may want to consider their needs in designing your site. Visit the Web site run by the Center for Applied Special Technology (http://www.cast.org) for more information.

Multimedia

Multimedia is commonly defined as communication achieved through the combination of two or more media—printed words, spoken words, music or other sound, images, animations, VRML, and interactivity. This area of communication is changing so fast that guidelines specific to a new technology may become out-of-date quickly. Use basic design and user interface knowledge in creating pages with multimedia.

Consider multimedia

Use multimedia when it will best meet your visitor's needs, such as:

- ❑ When a nonverbal medium is the natural way to express a concept
- ❑ To reach an audience that does not read or for whom reading is not a primary way of learning
- ❑ For an international audience
- ❑ To reinforce learning and aid retention through providing more than one channel
- ❑ To attract attention to an element on the page
- ❑ To provide feedback
- ❑ To show how things work

Keep the focus of your page

Visitors must know what to look at on your pages. Be sure that you do not confuse them by animation or sound that draws them away from the purpose of the page, rather than working with that purpose to make the page stronger. In addition, do not put so many things on one page that the user must decide what to focus on between conflicting elements.

Consider a simple slide show

Using the meta tag "refresh" you can create a simple slide show within your site or as an introduction to the site. Make a short series of simple files that load very quickly. Then set the timing in the tags. Each file loads, displays briefly, and then is replaced by the next file.

Consider simple animations using GIFs

Animated GIFs are simply a series of images combined into one file, much like a child's simple animation flip book. These images load more quickly than Java and provide effective simple animation.

Avoid repetitive animation

Avoid using small animations that provide constant movement in some part of the screen, unless it serves the purpose of your site. The human eye is drawn to constant movement, so your visitors have trouble concentrating on the content if, while reading, their eyes are constantly drawn to some repeating image.

Another problem with these animations is that they can interfere with a visitor's attempts to click on a link. The visitor must time their click in between the execution of the animation, which can cause extreme frustration.

Provide a way to turn off background sound

If you use a repeating background sound, provide a means of turning it off.

International Issues

Pay attention to the effects your content and design have on an international audience.

Think globally

Keep in mind that you are now communicating internationally. Design forms for an international audience. Consider other countries when setting the labels for and the length of address and phone fields.

Give the location of times

When indicating any time of day, indicate the time zone that you mean. Because not everyone understands time zone abbreviations in other countries, indicate what your target time is in scattered key sites around the world (New York, London, Sidney, Hong Kong, and so on). Also indicate whether you mean morning or afternoon. If you are using a 24-hour time system, say so.

Include state and country when indicating locations

Do not just say a city name when giving a location. For example, is Portland in Maine, Oregon, or England?

Avoid using hands as graphics

Any hand or finger position means something negative in some culture. It is best to avoid using hands as icons or graphical buttons.

Use English for an international audience

If you are writing in English and you are consciously writing for an international audience, keep your use of English simple and clear. Avoid unusual words, jargon, and clichés. Provide definitions and examples. Use graphics. Avoid humor, which is usually based in a specific culture—this includes avoiding visual jokes. Be cautious about using culturally based metaphors, such as football (USA) or rugby (England). A valuable site is "Words that could be confusing and embarrassing in the UK & US" at http:/www.dur.ac.uk/~dgl3djb/ukus.html.

12

Chapter

Online Support

Contents

Online Help

Wizards

There are many types of online support, for example: reference manuals, tutorials, context-sensitive help, and hypertext help systems. In this book we have included guidelines for standard online help systems and wizards.

Online Help

Online help systems are designed to support applications, although they can be used for other purposes, such as company procedures. Typically, users go to traditional help systems for information on how to perform specific tasks and actions. These guidelines support such systems.

Consider users' needs

People go to online help for quick and current answers to immediate problems. However, current research has shown that for most people, reading online is slower and harder than reading from paper. Consider the following points when deciding what types of information to put online.

Put online:

- ❑ Urgent information
- ❑ Specific information
- ❑ Information that changes frequently
- ❑ Reference information
- ❑ Documentation for the physically challenged

Don't put online:

- ❑ Installation information
- ❑ Information requiring lengthy or detailed reading
- ❑ Information needed offline

Consider users' experience level

If users aren't familiar with accessing online help, they typically look through the help index first. Users who are more experienced with online help often use the search feature first. Be aware of your users' experience levels and pay extra attention to the feature they will use most.

Limit the number of heading levels

Limit the number of heading levels and the amount of indentation. If you use too many indentations, you will require the user to use too many clicks to get to required information.

Keep text concise

Make it easy for your readers by eliminating all unnecessary words and detail. It is harder to read online text than hard copy text for the following reasons:

- ❑ A screen, especially a help panel, displays less information than a paper page.
- ❑ Text resolution online is less clear than on paper.
- ❑ Glare from monitors causes eye strain, especially if users are trying to read a lot of text.
- ❑ Farsighted people may have to tip their heads to read online, causing neck strain if they must do it for too long.

Keep topics short

Try not to make the users scroll to read the entire topic. Try to limit a topic to one help panel. Remember that your screen real estate is limited.

Create stand-alone chunks

A piece of information presented online must be able to stand alone. Write each topic so that it does not depend on a previous chunk of information for its meaning. Use one main idea for each topic and create links to related information.

Organize information for quick access and comprehension

Users must be able to find information within seconds. If they cannot find what they need quickly, they will stop using the online help. Use a hierarchical structure to give users clear mental models and help you organize your information. A table of contents is one example of hierarchical information. A thorough index is a must.

Provide links that allow users to move from topic to topic, following their own path to the information they need. Write a chunk of information once, but provide multiple paths to the same chunk. Allow users to access specific information directly by using a keyword search.

Be consistent

Consistency in the organization and presentation of information is important in all professional writing, but is especially important when writing for online use. Be consistent in all your user cues. For example, always use boldface and colors to cue the visitor to the same information. Always construct similar topics with the same information in the same order.

Use an active writing style

Use the active voice when writing online help. It creates stronger and shorter sentences than does the passive voice. Instead of "When the Search button is clicked, topics are displayed," use: "Click Search. From the Search dialog box, select your topic."

Use present tense to create more direct and powerful text. Instead of "When you click the Search button the topics will appear," use: "Click Search. The topics appear."

Address the reader directly. The informal pronoun "you" creates a friendlier tone and helps you avoid using gender-specific pronouns. It also helps you avoid writing in passive voice. Instead of: "The user has a number of actions he can take at this point," use: "Now you can take a number of actions."

Use color cautiously

Do not use color just to make things look pretty. Color should be used to cue users about specific information such as jump hot spots or warnings. Use color consistently across all parts of your help system.

Minimize the number of cues that users must remember. Use no more than three colors. Users will be trying to learn information from your help system and should not be bothered by having to struggle to remember what your cues mean.

Avoid problems with colorblindness and varying color displays by accompanying color with other character formatting, such as under-lining.

Wizards

Wizards break complicated tasks into small manageable chunks. They are series of dialog boxes with a controlled set of user actions at each step.

Consider wizards for critical tasks

If users must complete a critical task thoroughly, a wizard will ensure each substep is completed and in the correct order.

Consider wizards for infrequent and critical tasks

If a task is not performed very often and is important, using a wizard means users will not have to remember how to complete the task.

Consider wizards for tasks requiring complex decisions

If a task requires complex decision-making, a wizard helps break the decision down into manageable chunks and presents them in the cor-rect order.

Consider alternative formats

For some tasks you may choose to have a wizard as well as a regular series of screens and dialog boxes. As users get familiar with the task, they may prefer to skip the wizard and go right to the series of screens.

Chapter 13

Best Practices for Customizing, Implementing, and Maintaining Guidelines

Contents

You can use this book as a template for your own enterprise-wide guidelines. Although creating enterprise-wide guidelines seems like the greatest amount of work, how you implement and maintain them after you create them is just as important. After working with our clients over the last few years, we have developed our list of best practices for how to customize, implement, and maintain guidelines.

Whom to Involve

In order for guidelines to be successful, people must buy into them. The best way for people to buy into guidelines is to be involved in the process of customizing and implementing them. The most successful guidelines implementation strategies come from involving people at two levels: a core group level and a reviewer level.

Core Group

Your core group of guidelines task force members should be around six to eight people, and they should be representative of both developers and user groups within business units. This core group is responsible for:

- Making any changes to customize the guidelines
- Developing a rollout and implementation plan
- Implementing the rollout plan
- Deciding who should be the guidelines coordinator for maintenance and updating

The amount of time the core group puts in on the guidelines project and how long they need to be together depends on the extent of customization you are doing. It is typical for core group members to put in three to six hours per week for four to six weeks to customize and roll out guidelines. This is an average, since some weeks are busier than others.

The Reviewer Group

In addition to the six to eight core group members, you should decide on a larger group of reviewer members. You may have anywhere from eight to 20 members in your reviewer group. The more people you have, the more work you have, but the more buy-in you have. The reviewer group members have the following responsibilities:

- ❑ Reviewing drafts of a customized document
- ❑ Reviewing rollout plans and making comments
- ❑ Getting the word out when guidelines are available

Reviewer group members can expect to spend about two hours a week for about four weeks. This is a great role for people to play who are critical in the buy-in process.

What to Customize

Here are some of the changes and additions you may want to make.

Button Names

Consider adding to the list of reserved words for button names. Look at your existing systems or prototypes, talk to your developers and users, and decide on additional names you may want to add to the list. Decide on any button names you want to change or delete from the list.

Menu Bar Items

Consider choosing additional menu bar item if you repeatedly have action categories that occur across a lot of applications.

Tool Restrictions

If your current GUI programming tools do not allow you to follow some of the guidelines in this book, you will need to decide whether you are going to:

- ❑ Take out that guideline
- ❑ Leave it in with a note that your current environment cannot support it

Pictures and Screen Captures

One of the most powerful ways that you can customize the guidelines is to include some of your own real or prototype screens in place of, or in addition to, the graphics that are in this book. The more of your screens that you can provide, the better. This is not an all-or-none idea. You might use the screens provided in the files that accompany this book and incorporate ones of your own, or replace some of ours with some of yours.

Graphics

You may want to include particular graphics, for instance, toolbar graphics, corporate logos, or standard product images.

Contact Name and Phone Number

Identify a person to act as a contact for the guidelines. You may want to include this person's name and number in your version.

Feedback Form

You may want to include a form for users or developers to fill out and send in if they have feedback on a particular guideline or if they would like to suggest changes or additions to guidelines.

Next Version

If you have a date when you expect an updated version of guidelines to come out, you may want to include that in your guidelines.

A Cover Page

Create your own cover page with your company name, logo, and version number.

Project Planning for Customizing Guidelines

Here are some milestone points in a guidelines plan. Adjust these to best fit your own process.

Initial steps

Your initial steps of customizing guidelines are to:

- ❑ Decide who will be in the core group
- ❑ Decide who will be in the reviewer group
- ❑ Have all core group members review this guidelines document

Have a Kickoff Meeting

Have a kickoff meeting to decide the following:

- ❑ Scope of guidelines
- ❑ General process milestone dates
- ❑ Roles and responsibilities
- ❑ Required time commitment
- ❑ Suggestions for reviewer group that have not been completed

Assign a Task Force Coordinator

It is the coordinator's job to get all the information to everyone, confirm meetings, take notes, and so on.

Assign Research Jobs

Decide how you want to proceed with customization decisions. Consider assigning different jobs to different people or teams on your core group. For example, you may want to split your core group into three groups of two. Assign different topics to teams for researching customization decisions. Another team might be responsible for coming up with the initial rollout plan.

Often guidelines task forces will divide up this book and have each team come back to the group with suggestions for customization.

Once you have agreed upon what customization you are going to do, assign rewriting, rewording, and taking new screen pictures to the teams. Creating and shooting screen pictures is probably the most time consuming part of the project. If you give a person or a team this responsibility, make sure they have plenty of help and time to do it.

Research Media Decisions

Have one team check out your options for creating the document.

❑ Who is designing and printing the cover page?
❑ Are you printing a hard copy?
❑ What tools will you use to take screen captures?
❑ Will the paper document contain color?
❑ What kind of bindings will you use?
❑ How much printing lead time do you need?
❑ What tools will you use to put the document online?

Create a New Draft

Once you have gathered all the customized changes, create a new draft of the guidelines.

Send the Draft Out to Reviewers

Now is the time to send your draft to the reviewer group. Make sure you give them instructions as to what you want them to do.

Some suggestions might be to have them identify any guidelines that they find hard to understand or that would be hard to implement. You may want to suggest to them that you are going to listen carefully to all their suggestions, although you may not be able to implement all of them immediately.

Get Feedback and Decide What to Act On

Once you get feedback from your core group and your reviewer group on the draft, you need to decide what changes you are actually going to implement and then make them.

Implementing and Maintaining Guidelines

In order for your guidelines to be successful, people must know they exist and be encouraged to use them. As early in the process as possible, you should put together an implementation plan to identify how you are going to announce and get guidelines out. Companies who succeed in implementing guidelines effectively are companies who plan the introduction of the guidelines.

The particular methods you use to implement guidelines need to be adjusted for your own corporate culture. As a starting point, think about how change has occurred successfully in your organization in the past. If there have been recent ways of rolling out new technologies or new ideas, you may want to copy the methods used.

Establish a Clear home and Coordinator

People always have questions about guidelines. Make sure it is clear to them who and where to call for help. There should be a specific person to call, not just a department. People are more likely to make a call when there is a name and number, not just a department or group. You want people to call. It means that they are clearing up confusion.

Do not rotate this duty among a group. One person needs to be hearing all the comments. One person needs to know the guidelines backwards and forwards and have the document as a major part of their work. Identify one other person as backup in case the guidelines person is not available.

The guidelines person should collect suggestion forms and other comments from the users of the guidelines document. Then you will be ready when it is time for a new version.

Be Ready for Contact

When people call with questions about guidelines, the time is ripe to help them with design. Your guidelines coordinator could be your in-house interface design specialist. So think carefully about who the co-ordinator should be and provide them with the training and support they need to give advice above and beyond the documented guidelines.

Actively Solicit Support

Developers are not the only people that need to know and understand guidelines. Business unit managers, users involved in design teams, contractors in place, or vendors you are considering all need to be aware of and familiar with your guidelines at some level. In addition to familiarity, you will need buy-in and support from these groups in order for guidelines to be successful.

Once guidelines are in place you cannot assume your work is over. You need to constantly lobby, get support from, and give support to everyone who is impacted by the guidelines. Try to get support all the way up and down the line from you. Consider education and training sessions for a wide range of people. These sessions might be different from what the developers receive, but they are equally important.

Plan to Revise and Update

Although you would probably like to create guidelines once and have them work forever, this is not reality. Plan for change ahead of time. Decide when and how often you will review your guidelines. A new version may be necessary every six to 12 months. Talk about reviews ahead of time so people expect that there will be changes.

Create a suggestion form in paper and perhaps online that people can fill out when they have questions or suggestions about guidelines. These will let you know which guidelines need to be changed or clarified.

Decide on Compliance Reviews

Are applications required to go through a guidelines compliance review, or is compliance only voluntary? If you have a review process, make sure it happens iteratively and early. It is frustrating for developers to make changes late in their interface design. The earlier you catch compliance problems, the more willing everyone is to make the changes.

Make compliance reviews part of standard operating procedures if you have them. If people know there will be one, they will not be as defensive as if you spring it on them suddenly. They need to get used to planning ahead for a compliance review.

Decide How to Handle Exceptions

People will sometimes have legitimate reasons for wanting an exception to a guideline for their particular application. Decide ahead of time how you will handle these requests. You should design your guidelines so that they work 80 percent of the time. This means that you expect exceptions. If a particular guideline gets exception requests often, it is time to consider changing it.

Provide Training

You will need to provide training on the guidelines. Do not rely on people just reading them. Consider having an interface design class that also teaches your guidelines. People learn some of the reasons behind the guidelines, and get to use them right away in the class. The participants remember the guidelines better, and at the end of class they are familiar with the document. It is especially crucial that outside contractors get training in your guidelines. Chances are they have been trained in someone else's guidelines and need to be retrained.

Develop a Grandfather Clause

You cannot expect applications that have been delivered to automatically go through a major re-write just to comply with guidelines. In addition, you cannot expect all applications to schedule a new version to coincide with your new guidelines.

Meet with teams that have existing applications and come to a clear understanding of what will happen and when. It is reasonable to expect that when they do a major new version they will include at least some significant guidelines compliance. Get a clear agreement as to what is a major new version, and what is significant. Before they start their version update, agree upon a list of guideline changes they will incorporate. They need to be able to plan ahead.

Give up the goal of perfection. You will probably not be able to have all applications exactly compliant on the same version of guidelines. Spend your energy getting as many applications as you can as compliant as possible. Concentrate on new applications and enhancements.

Make a plan with feedback from the teams, come to agreement with teams, and then be firm. It will only confuse everyone if you waffle. It needs to be clear to all what the grandfathering rules are.

Remember the Tradeoffs

You must remember and remind your design teams that interface design is a constant game of making tradeoffs, and guidelines especially so. We are trading off what might be ideal for a particular screen or application with the benefit of consistency across screens, across applications, and industry-wide.

Don't Assume Guidelines Are ALL

Guidelines are a critical part of effective interface design, but they are not all of it. There are critical interface design decisions that need to be made even after guidelines are followed. Guideline compliance does not replace interface design. Are you involving users in enough places in the interface design process? Do you have an interface design process? Do your developers know how to do effective interface design?

A

Appendix

List of Guidelines

Contents

Structure

Interaction

Presentation

Internet and Intranet

Online Support

Structure

Primary and Secondary Windows

Use cascading windows.

Avoid horizontal scrolling.

Size secondary windows to fit data.

Place pop-up windows in the center of the action.

Dialog Boxes

Use modal dialogs for closure.

Use modeless dialogs for continuing work.

Tabs

Consider tab cards for discrete categories of information.

Tab card sets should relate to an object.

Consider tab cards when the order of information varies.

Make sure the information is independent.

Use only one to two rows of tabs.

Use a master window or dialog box.

Place buttons appropriately.

Be consistent.

Choose a horizontal or vertical flow.

Menus

Word menu items carefully.

Change menus as you need.

Use initial caps.

Follow industry standards for menus.

Menu Bars

Match menu bars to the users' work flow.

Give critical or frequent tasks even weight.

Place application-specific menu items where they fit.

Use only one word for menu bar items.

Use only one line for the menu bar.

Do not gray out menu bar items.

Menu bar items should always activate a drop-down menu.

Drop-Down Menus

Use more than one drop-down menu item.

Use unique drop-down items.

Limit drop-down menus to one screen in length.

Put frequent or critical items at the top.

Use separator bars.

Use no more than two levels of cascading.

Use ellipses (...) to denote dialogs.

Use industry standard keyboard equivalents.

Use accelerators sparingly.

Use consistent accelerators.

Pop-Up Menus

Use pop-up menus for specific options.

Use redundant interactions.

Roll-Up Menus

Use roll-up menus for frequent actions.

Toolbars

Make toolbars consistent.

Make only active items available.

Allow users to move some toolbars.

Allow users to toggle toolbars on and off.

Allow customizing.

Use buttons with a purpose.

Use tooltips.

Group like items.

Relationship between Toolbars, Command Buttons, and Menus

Use toolbars for frequent actions across screens.

Use toolbars to supplement menus.

Use toolbars in place of some menu items.

Interaction

Command Buttons

Use command buttons only for frequent or critical immediate actions.

Label buttons carefully.

Label buttons consistently.

Use industry standards for labels.

Consider replacing the OK button with a specific term.

Size buttons relative to each other.

Separate buttons from the rest of the dialog box.

Group buttons together.

Place buttons consistently.

Match button position to the use of the window.

Position limited action buttons where needed.

Order buttons consistently.

Use ellipses (...) to indicate that input is needed.

Gray out unavailable buttons.

Assign a nondestructive default button.

Option Buttons

Use option buttons for one choice.

Label option buttons descriptively.

Group option buttons together and label them.

Align option buttons vertically.

Limit option buttons to six or fewer.

Choose an order.

Avoid binary option buttons.

Check Boxes

Use check boxes for choosing more than one option.

Use check boxes for toggling.

Label check boxes descriptively.

Group and label check boxes.

Align check boxes vertically.

Limit check boxes to ten or fewer.

Choose an order.

Do not use Select All or Deselect All check boxes.

Text Boxes

Use a border to indicate data entry.

Show display-only data without a box.

Gray out temporarily protected fields.

Use box length to signify approximate data length.
Align text boxes.
Group text boxes.
Label all text boxes.
Place labels to the left.
Align text box labels to the left.
Place a colon after text box labels.

List Boxes

Use list boxes for long lists.
Use list boxes for dynamic data.
Show three to eight items at a time.
Label each list box.
Use filters for large lists.
Use drop-down list boxes to save space.
Use a combination list box to allow users to type in an option.

Multiple Selection List Boxes

Use a multiple selection list box instead of check boxes.
Consider instructions for multiple selection list boxes.
Consider a selection summary box.
Consider multiple selection checklists.
Consider Select All or Deselect All buttons.

Tables and Grids

Use tables for comparisons among data.
Use grids for multiple data entry.
Label columns.
Use row labels if necessary.
Left justify labels.

Spin Boxes

Use spin boxes for limited cycling.

Combine spin boxes with text boxes.

Sliders

Use sliders for visually choosing values.

Use sliders for large data ranges.

Display results.

Allow data entry.

Allow the use of arrows for small increments.

Tree Views

Use tree views when hierarchy is important.

Use tree views for more advanced users.

Do not use tree views to replace menus, home bases, or launch pads.

Presentation

Screen Layout

Organize windows and dialogs to match work flow.

Use an appropriate amount of information.

Find a home base.

Organize information within a window.

Choose a horizontal or vertical flow.

Group similar data.

Minimize different margins.

Fonts

Use a sans serif font.

Do not use italics or underlining.

Avoid using colored fonts.

Use bold for emphasis.

Avoid changing font size.

Use at least an eight point font.

Minimize the number of different fonts.

Color Choices and Combinations

Use color to get attention.

Use color purposefully.

Combine color with redundant highlighting.

Be aware of color blindness.

Watch out for color customizing.

Use colors consistently.

Use color in toolbars sparingly.

Follow cultural color meanings.

Use light backgrounds for main areas.

Avoid red and blue combinations.

Avoid blue text.

Use enough contrast.

Avoid light text on dark.

Use grayware first.

Let users customize color.

Use color palettes.

Provide a reset.

Consider showing results before setting.

Designing or Choosing Graphics

Use graphics for a purpose.

Use button images as shortcuts.

Use graphics when a picture is worth....

Use graphics for international use.

Decide on an approach.

Develop a cohesive set.

Include just enough detail for recognition.

Watch out for picture size.

Use standard graphics.

Consider changing the graphic's state.

Be consistent.

Avoid words.

Get appropriate help.

Test your graphics.

Charts and Graphs

Use graphs to show relationships.

Use bar graphs for categories.

Use special effects carefully.

Use pie charts for part-to-whole relationships.

Use line charts for continuous data.

Choose appropriate scales.

Consider displaying specific values.

Use visual coding on graphs.

Use legends for complicated graphs.

Label graphs and data.

Use primary colors to show differences.

Use red cautiously.

Use close colors to show transition.

Use light backgrounds for tables.

Use monochromatic backgrounds for graphs.

Internet and Intranet

Site Design

Provide meaningful content.

Give people a reason to bookmark your site.

Keep usability a high priority.

Create a unified design.

Use a hierarchical structure.

Consider a grabber page.

Use a home page as the menu for the rest of the site.

Provide redundancy in home page menus.

Use submenus for large sites.

Understand the bandwidths of your target audience.

Keep your file size small.

Provide a printing option for long pages.

Provide cues.

Use a site map to indicate the relationships of information.

Make each item in a site map a link to the topic.

Use hierarchical text-based maps.

Consider image maps for graphical navigation.

Prepare your pages for external search engines.

Add a search engine to your site.

Design for multiple browsing environments.

Navigation

Follow the three clicks rule.

Use progressive disclosure.

Make navigation cues consistent.

In a large site, provide two levels of navigation.

Don't tie navigation or content to graphics alone.

Provide text links to your pages.

Use links carefully.

Make links to substantive content.

Be sure the link text is clear.

Make only a few words the active link.

Be careful with Previous, Back, Next, and Forward.

Avoid "Click Here."

Avoid "Return To."

Be sure visitors can distinguish between visited and new links.

Annotate all links to large files.

Use internal links for long pages.

Maintain correct internal links.

Bury external links.

Check and correct external links frequently.

Page Layout

Place the most important content at the top.

Include standard page elements.

Keep the home page to one screen.

Pay attention to probable page breaks.

Decide on long pages versus short pages.

Break a long page up into smaller units.

Use a grid.

Consider using tables.

Keep line lengths short.

Use tables to keep lines short.

Consider using style sheets.

Use enough white space.

Use enough horizontal spacing.

Keep images and related text close to each other.

Use horizontal rules sparingly.

Group the items in a form.

Group long lists.

Use hanging indents.

Consider the design of bullets.

Minimize vertical scrolling.

Do not use horizontal scrolling.

Page Titles and Headings

Make each title unique and meaningful.

Give each page a title.

Use a name that labels the entire site and the specific page.

Use headings to help visitors scan for information.

In long documents include document and chapter names on each page.

Frames and Windows

Use frames with caution.

Do not use multiple windows unless they add functionality.

Limit the number of windows or frames to two.

Consider frames for global elements.

Consider frames for pop-up text.

Use frames to keep lines short.

Watch out for window size.

Graphics

Use graphics for a purpose.

Use text with graphics.

Use alternative text.

Reuse images.

Use images to help with navigation.

Use graphics to represent content areas.

Use graphics for special headline fonts.

Use graphics for lists.

Remember the many limitations of images.

Use thumbnails.

Size the image to fit on the screen.

Use as small an image as possible.

Simplify drawings.

Use a low source image.

Use interlaced GIFs.

Don't put borders on the image in a drawing program.

Use transparent images over a patterned background.

Specify image dimensions in HTML.

Remember that search engines ignore images.

Backgrounds

Use light-colored backgrounds of low intensity.

Avoid patterned backgrounds.

Pick a random background pattern.

Avoid watermarked text.

Use a background color when you use a background image.

Remember that visitors can set a default background color.

Test backgrounds.

Color

Maintain high contrast.

Use large areas of uniform color.

Reduce color depth.

Use colors from the 216 supported by most browsers.

Use the same palette for all images on a page.

Avoid dithering except in photos.

Test colors.

Fonts

Use sans serif fonts for online reading.

Use bold text for emphasis only.

Use italics with care.

Do not use underlining.

Design for changes in font sizes.

Use font tags to control text size.

Use fonts to express corporate identity.

Readability

Write for visitor control.

Say it once, quickly.

Design for scanning.

Write in short chunks.

Create clear concise labels for text chunks.

Use an active writing style.

Write positive messages.

Use normal writing conventions for lists.

Netiquette

Keep information current.

Put a "Last Updated" date in your footer.

Give visitors something to do while they wait.

Provide a way for visitors to talk back to you.

Answer your mail.

Don't use others' material or code without permission and credit.

Ask permission before linking to someone's site.

Get permission to use trademarks and logos.

Indicate that your information is copyrighted.

Be careful about humor.

Consider the needs of disabled visitors.

Multimedia

Consider multimedia.

Keep the focus of your page.

Consider a simple slide show.

Consider simple animations using GIFs.

Avoid repetitive animation.

Provide a way to turn off background sound.

International Issues

Think globally.

Give the location of times.

Include state and country when indicating locations.

Avoid using hands as graphics.

Use English for an international audience.

Online Support

Online Help

Consider users' needs.

Consider users' experience levels.

Limit the number of heading levels.

Keep text concise.

Keep topics short.

Create stand-alone chunks.

Organize information for quick access and comprehension.

Be consistent.

Use an active writing style.

Use color cautiously.

Wizards

Consider wizards for critical tasks.

Consider wizards for infrequent and critical tasks.

Consider wizards for tasks requiring complex decisions.

Consider alternative formats.

B

Appendix

For More Information

Interface Design

Allen, C. Dennis. (1995, May). Succeeding as a clandestine change agent. *Communications of the ACM, 38* (5).

Balasubramanian, V. (1995, October). Designing in the real world. *Interactions.*

Bannon, Liam J. (1995, September). The politics of design: Representing work. *Communications of the ACM, 38* (9).

Bauersfield, Penny. (1994). *Software by design.* M & T Books.

Bias, Randolph G., & Deborah J. Mayhew (Eds.). (1994). *Cost justifying usability.* Academic Press.

Borchers, Jan, Oliver Duessen, & Clemens Knorzer. (1995, October). Getting it across. *SIGCHI Bulletin, 27* (4).

Carroll, John M. (Ed.). (1994). *Scenario-based design.* New York: John Wiley & Sons.

Carroll, John M. (1995, April). The scenario perspective on system development. *Interactions.*

Charette, Robert N. (1995, May). How to create a successful failure. *Communications of the ACM, 38* (5).

comp.human-factors. An interface design news group.

Dayton, Tom, et al. (1993, July). Skills needed by user-centered design practitioners in real software development environments: Report on the CHI '92 workshop. *SIGCHI Bulletin, 25* (3).

Dumas, Joseph S., & Janice C. Redish. (1994). *A practical guide to usability testing.* Ablex Publishing Corporation.

Galitz, Wilbert O. (1994). *It's time to clean your windows: Designing GUIs that work.* New York: John Wiley & Sons.

Genter, Don, and Jakob Nielson. (1996, August). The anti-mac interface. *Communications of the ACM, 39* (8).

Greenbaum, J., & M. Kyng (Eds.). (1991). *Design at work.* Erlbaum.

Helander, Martin (Ed.). (1988). *Handbook of human-computer interaction.* North Holland.

Holtzblatt, Karen, & Hugh Beyer. (1993, October). Making customer-centered design work for teams. *Communications of the ACM, 36* (10).

Horton, William. (1994). *The icon book.* New York: John Wiley & Sons.

Human Factors and Ergonomics Society
PO Box 1369
Santa Monica, CA 90406-1369
Phone: 310-394-1811
Fax: 310-394-2410

Interactions Magazine. Call ACM at 212-626-0500 for subscription information.

Kano, Nadine. (1995 March/April). Putting on an international interface. *Microsoft Developer Network News.*

Kyng, Morten. (1995, September). Making representations work. *Communications of the ACM, 38* (9).

Landauer, Thomas K. (1995). *The trouble with computers.* Massachusetts Institute of Technology.

Laurel, Brenda. (1990). *The Art of human-computer interface design.* Addison-Wesley.

Madsen, Kim Halskov. (1994, December). A guide to metaphorical design. *Communications of the ACM, 37* (12).

Mullett, Kevin, & Darrell Sano. (1995). *Designing visual interfaces.* Sun Microsystems, Inc.

Nielsen, Jakob, & Robert L. Mack (Eds.). (1994). *Usability inspection methods.* New York: John Wiley & Sons.

Norman, Don. (1988). *The design of everyday things.* Basic Books.

Norman, Don. (1993). *Things that make us smart.* Addison-Wesley.

Norman, Don. (1992). *Turn signals are the facial expressions of automobiles.* Addison-Wesley.

Preece, Jenny. (1994). *Human computer interaction.* Addison-Wesley.

Popowicz, Alison. (1995, October). Collecting user information on a limited budget. *SIGCHI Bulletin, 27* (4).

Resources for HCI education. (1995, April). *Interactions.*

Rettig, Marc. (1995, April). Gaps. *Interactions.*

Rettig, Marc. (1994, April). Prototyping for tiny fingers. *Communications of the ACM, 37* (4).

Rubin, Jeffrey. (1994). *Handbook of usability testing: How to plan, design, and conduct effective tests.* New York: John Wiley & Sons.

SIGCHI (Special Interest Group for Computer Human Interaction)
Association for Computing Machinery
11 West 42nd St.
New York, NY 10036
212-869-7440

Trower, Randy. (1994). *Creating a well-designed user interface.* Produced by University Video Communications, directed by Randy Trower. 64 min. Videocassette.

Tufte, Edward R. (1994). *Envisioning information.* Graphic Press.

Usability Professionals Association
Amy Stewart
4020 McEwen
Suite 105
Dallas, TX 75244-5019
Phone: 214-233-9107 ext. 206
Fax: 214-490-4219
UPAdallas@aol.com
http://www.Upssoc.org

Weinschenk, Susan. (1995, October). Intelligent GUI design: Six critical mindset shifts. *Data Management Review, 5* (9).

Weston, Rusty. (1995, June). Pushing the limits of RAD. *Open Computing.*

White, Jan V. (1990). *Color for the electronic age.* Watson Guptill.

White, Jan V. (1988). *Graphic design for the electronic age.* Watson Guptill.

Wiklund, Michael E. (Ed.). (1994). *Usability in practice.* Academic Press.

Guidelines

Kobara, Shiz. (1991). *Visual design with OSF/Motif.* Addison-Wesley.

Macintosh human interface guidelines. (1992). Apple Computer.

Marcus, Aaron, Nick Smilonich, & Lynne Thompson. (1995). *The cross-GUI handbook for multiplatform user interface design.* Addison-Wesley.

Object-oriented interface design. (1992, December). IBM Common User Access Guidelines. IBM, QUE.

Open look graphical user interface application style guidelines. Sun Microsystems.

OSF/Motif programmer's guide and OSF/Motif style guide. (1991). Prentice Hall.

The windows interface guidelines for software design. (1995). Microsoft Press.

Weinschenk, Susan, & Sarah Yeo. (1995). *Guidelines for enterprise-wide GUI design.* New York: John Wiley & Sons.

Online Help and Documentation

Horton, William. (1994). *Illustrating computer documentation.* New York: John Wiley & Sons.

Horton, William. (1994). *Designing and writing online documentation,* 2nd ed. New York: John Wiley & Sons.

Kearsley, Greg. (1988). *On-line help systems.* Albex Publishing.

McKendree, Jean, Will Reader, & Nick Hammon. (1995, July). The homeopathic fallacy in learning from hypertext. *Interactions.*

Mischel, Jim, & Jeff Duntemann. (1994). *The developers guide to WINHELP.EZE, Harnessing the Windows help engine.* New York: John Wiley & Sons.

Nichols, Michelle Corbin, & Robert R. Berry. (1996, August). Design principles for multi-window online information systems:

Conclusions from research, applications, and experience. *Technical Communication, Journal of the Society for Technical Communication*, *43* (3), 244-254.

Pruitt, Steve. (1996, Spring). The future of WinHelp. *HyperViews*, newsletter of the STC Online Information Professional Interest Committee, *2* (1).

Society for Technical Communication
901 N. Stuart St., Suite 904
Arlington, VA 22203-1854
Phone: 703-522-4114
Fax: 703-522-2075
BBS: 703-522-3299

Welinski, Joe, et al. (1996, Spring/Summer). Various articles on Netscape and Microsoft plans for HTML help, intranets, conversion tools, and writing hypertext. *The WinHelp Journal*, *2* (3/4).

The WinHelp Newsgroup can be found at comp.os.ms-windows.programmer.winhlp. You can subscribe to the WinHelp Mail List by sending the following unsigned e-mail message on the Internet:
Address: listserv@admin.humberc.on.ca
Message: sub winhlp-L

Web Design

Information on the Internet changes rapidly. Use the following links, but supplement them by conducting your own search for key terms so that you find the latest Web articles.

Berners-Lee, Tim. *Style guide for online hypertext.* <http://www.w3.org/pub/WWW/Provider/Style/Overview.html>. 1995.

Center for Applied Special Technology <http://www.cast.org/>

Hoft, Nancy L. (1995). *International technical communication: How to export information about high technology.* New York: John Wiley & Sons.

Horton, William, et al. (1996). *Web page design cookbook.* New York: John Wiley & Sons.

Horton, William. (1995, November). Why should I use multimedia? *Ergoglyphics, about communication for work that works,* <http://www. horton.com/brochure/ergo/ergo.htm>.

Levine, Rick. (1996, August 2). *Guide to Web style.* <http://www.sun. com/styleguide/tables/Welcome.html>.

Lynch, Peter J. (1996, January). *C/AIM Web Style Manual.* <http://info. med.yale.edu/caim/StyleManual_Top.HTML>.

Nielsen, Jakob. Alert Box columns, *Sun Microsystems.* http://www.sun. com:80/columns/alertbox.html>.

Sano, Darrrell. (1996). *Designing large-scale Web sites: A visual design methodology.* New York: John Wiley & Sons.

Siegel, David. (1996). *Creating killer Web sites.* Indianapolis: Hayden Books.

Siegel, David. (1996, August). *Creating killer web sites.* <http://www. killersites.com/>.

Siegel, David. (1996, August). *The David Siegel project.* <http://www. dsiegel.com/home.html>.

Weinman, Lynda. (1996) *<designing web graphics>.* Indianapolis: New Riders Publishing.

Weinman, Lynda. *Lynda's homegurrrl page.* <http://www.lynda.com>.

Wilson, Dr. Ralph F. (1996, August). *12 Web page design decisions your business or organization will need to make.* <http://www.wilsonweb. com/rfwilson/smalbus/12design.htm>.

Appendix C

Forms, Tables, and Checklists

Contents

User Profile Form

Task Detail Table

Usability Specifications Table

Analysis Checklist

Object-Action Table

Object-Metaphor-
Representation Table

Action Table

Knowledge and Skills Table

Support Planning Table

Design Checklist

Construction Checklist

Usability Testing Checklist

User Profile Form

Application:

Potential Users:

Hardware Experience:

Software and Interface Experience:

Experience with Similar Applications:

Task Experience:

Frequency of Use:

Key Interface Design Requirements that Profile Suggests:

Task Detail Table

Task #	Task	Frequency	Display Requirements	Input Requirements	Comments

Usability Specifications Table

Measurable Behavior	Criteria	Key Elements	Users

	Analysis Checklist
✔	**Step**
	Identify current state and scope
	Consider work in progress
	Decide on the scope of the analysis
	Define interface design constraints
	Develop user profiles
	Gather data
	Validate user profiles
	Gather task data
	Document the current tasks
	Decide how to document the current tasks
	Document current tasks
	Validate current task documents
	Document problems and opportunities
	Document problems and opportunities
	Validate problems and opportunities
	Describe future tasks
	Describe future tasks
	Validate future task descriptions
	Develop usability specifications
	Develop specifications
	Validate specifications
	Develop use case scenarios
	Develop use case scenarios
	Validate use case scenarios
	Test

Object-Action Table		
Object/Sub-Object	Attributes	User Actions

Object-Metaphor-Representation Table

Object/Sub-Object	Metaphor	Representation

Action Table				
Action	Command Button	Toolbar	Menu	Other GUI Widget

Knowledge & Skills Table	
Knowledge/Skill	Users Already Possess?

Support Planning Table						
Deficiency	Getting Started Tutorial	Online Help	User Guide	Quick Ref Card	Online Cue Cards	Other

Design Checklist	
✔	**Step**
	Choose major user objects
	Identify objects from analysis documents
	Identify object attributes
	Identify user actions on task objects
	Select metaphors and representations
	Storyboard the major user objects and metaphors
	Create a high-level interface design
	Select/adapt a style
	Identify main windows and related user actions
	Identify home bases and launching pads
	Identify how user access main windows
	Assign user actions for main windows
	Create design mockups
	Review and revise the high-level design
	Test
	Develop the support plan
	Identify user knowledge and skill deficiencies
	Map the support plan

Construction Checklist	
✔	Step
	Develop the hi-fi computer prototype
	Conduct design reviews
	Revise prototype
	Conduct usability tests
	Revise prototype
	Create a User Interface Design Description

Usability Testing Checklist	
✔	Step
	Identify the scope
	Decide on the type of media
	Decide on interaction
	Decide on the test environment
	Review and confirm usability specifications
	Choose participants
	Plan and conduct the test
	Create test scenarios
	Develop a usability test plan
	Create materials
	Run a pilot test
	Conduct the test
	Analyze and report test results
	Develop a preliminary report
	Develop a final report
	Prepare a presentation

How to Use the Files on CD-ROM

Contents

Using the Online Files

Using the Customizable Files

User Assistance and Information

Table D.1 Files included on the CD-ROM.

Filename	Format	Description
Book.dot	Word 7.0 template	Template for the guidelines customizable files
Structur.doc	Word 7.0 document	Chapter 8, Structure
Interact.doc	Word 7.0 document	Chapter 9, Interaction
Present.doc	Word 7.0 document	Chapter 10, Presentation
Internet.doc	Word 7.0 document	Chapter 11, Internet and Intranet
Forms.doc	Word 7.0 document	Appendix C, Forms, Tables, and Checklists
Main.pdf	Adobe Acrobat file	Title page and main contents for online guidelines
Structur.pdf	Adobe Acrobat file	Chapter 8, Structure
Interact.pdf	Adobe Acrobat file	Chapter 9, Interaction
Present.pdf	Adobe Acrobat file	Chapter 10, Presentation
Internet.pdf	Adobe Acrobat file	Chapter 11, Internet and Intranet

The CD-ROM contains the guideline chapters in both customizable Word 7.0 files and Adobe 3.0 online files. The Adobe Acrobat Reader 3.0 is included on the CD-ROM and needs to be installed before you can access the Adobe online files. Appendix C, Forms, Tables, and Checklists, is also included in Word 7.0 format. Table D.1 lists the names and descriptions of the files that we have created and put on the CD-ROM.

The CD-ROM also includes files for the Adobe Acrobat Reader.

Using the Online Files

Before you can view the guideline files online, you need to install the Adobe Acrobat Reader by using the appropriate setup.exe file on the CD-ROM.

To use our online files, you can either copy all of the *.pdf files to your hard drive or use them from the CD-ROM. If you choose to copy the files to your hard drive:

❏ Check your hard drive free space. The online files total 8.96MB.

❏ All of the *.pdf files must be copied to X:\ONLINE, where X = your hard drive letter. The links in the files will not work if the files are put in any other directory path.

After you have installed the Reader, you can view the online files by opening the Main.pdf file. This file contains the main table of contents and links to all the other guideline files.

Using the Customizable Files

If you would like to customize the guidelines provided in Word 7.0 format, copy the *.doc files to your hard drive. The Word template, Book.dot, is also included on the CD-ROM. This template includes all the styles for the guideline files. If you want to continue to use a template for these files, book.dot must be copied to your MSOffice\Templates directory. You can then open the template and modify the styles as you wish (see Table D.2 for descriptions of the styles). When you open the guideline files, Word will automatically update them to reflect any modifications you have made to the template. (Note: The

Table D.2 The styles used in the customizable files.

Style Name	*Used for*
Heading1	Chapter headings
Heading2	Section headings
Heading3	Guideline headings
BodyText	Body text
BulletList	Bullet lists
Numberlist	Numbered lists
TableHeading	Table headings
TableText	Table text
GraphicCaption	Figure and table captions
Header	Page header
Footer	Page footer

files will not automatically update if they are open when you make changes to the template. You would need to close and reopen the files in this case.)

User Assistance and Information

The software accompanying this book is being provided as is without warranty or support of any kind. Should you require basic installation assistance, or if your media is defective, please call our product support number at (212) 850-6194 weekdays between 9 AM and 4 PM Eastern Standard Time. Or, we can be reached via e-mail at: **wprtusw @wiley.com**.

To place additional orders or to request information about other Wiley products, please call (800) 879-4539.

Index